FORGERS AND THIEVES

The Association for Research into Crimes against Art Books
Series Editor: Noah Charney

The Association for Research into Crimes against Art (ARCA) was founded in 2009 by Noah Charney as an international, nongovernmental organization that works to promote scholarly research in the study of art crime and cultural heritage protection. The first organization of its type, ARCA seeks to identify emerging and underexamined trends related to the study of art crime and to develop strategies that advocate for the responsible stewardship of our collective artistic and archaeological heritage. It aims to bridge the gap between the practical and theoretical by fostering collaboration among all diverse and relevant entities: foreign and domestic law enforcement officials, security consultants, academics, lawyers, archaeologists, insurance specialists, criminologists, art historians, conservators, and other parties who wish to learn the surprising and interesting ways that different professions overlap with, or are impacted by, art and heritage crime. At the most basic level, ARCA seeks to identify emerging and underexamined trends related to art crime.

ARCA advances its mission through its professional development training programs, its research, publications, capacity building, and public outreach. As an interdisciplinary group, ARCA works with scholars and allied professionals in the fields of law, criminal justice, security, museum studies, art history, archaeology, and cultural resource management at the local, national, and international level in order to foster an exchange of knowledge and the advancement of this specialized field.

ARCA is the go-to research group in the field—featured in the *New York Times*, *National Geographic*, the *Washington Post*, the *Guardian*, an Amazon Prime documentary—leading an influencer campaign for Samsung and even making an appearance in Dan Brown's novel *Inferno*.

Similarly, ARCA works to improve the collective relationship with the past by leveraging the knowledge and influence of professionals, patrons, and the public in protecting the world's common artistic patrimony. It also produces the *Journal of Art Crime*, an interdisciplinary and international, peer-reviewed journal of scholarly work in art crime research that is published twice a year.

This book series, a collaboration between ARCA and Rowman & Littlefield, seeks to establish the publishing series of record for scholarship on the multidisciplinary field of art crime.

For more information about ARCA, see https://www.artcrimeresearch.org/.

FORGERS AND THIEVES

The Shadowlands of Art Crime

NOAH CHARNEY

ROWMAN & LITTLEFIELD
Lanham • Boulder • New York • London

Published by Rowman & Littlefield
An imprint of The Rowman & Littlefield Publishing Group, Inc.
4501 Forbes Boulevard, Suite 200, Lanham, Maryland 20706
www.rowman.com

86-90 Paul Street, London EC2A 4NE

British Library Cataloguing in Publication Information Available

Library of Congress Cataloging-in-Publication Data

Names: Charney, Noah, author.
Title: Forgers and thieves : the shadowlands of art crime / Noah Charney.
Description: Lanham : Rowman & Littlefield, [2025] | Series: Association for Research into Crimes against Art books | Includes index.
Identifiers: LCCN 2024033043 (print) | LCCN 2024033044 (ebook) | ISBN 9798881802622 (cloth) | ISBN 9798881802639 (paperback) | ISBN 9798881802646 (epub)
Subjects: LCSH: Art--Forgeries. | Art thefts.
Classification: LCC N8790 .C474 2025 (print) | LCC N8790 (ebook) | DDC 364.16/35--dc23/eng/20240821
LC record available at https://lccn.loc.gov/2024033043
LC ebook record available at https://lccn.loc.gov/2024033044

™ The paper used in this publication meets the minimum requirements of American National Standard for Information Sciences—Permanence of Paper for Printed Library Materials, ANSI/NISO Z39.48-1992.

To Lynda Albertson and Edgar Tijhuis, for leading and believing in ARCA

Contents

Preface

In March 2019, ARCA (Association for Research into Crimes against Art) launched a successful Kickstarter campaign to raise scholarship funds for students to study in our summer program, and also to launch an ARCA Publications imprint that would release books on the subject of art crime. Such a focused publisher on art crime did not exist at the time, and ARCA, a research group on art crime that I founded in 2006 and the pioneer in this field of academic study, sought to fill that gap. The campaign led to the modest release of four books. But then the pandemic arrived and what momentum the project had wound to a halt, as did so much of the planet at the time.

I've since published more than twenty books, seven of them and counting with Rowman & Littlefield, and developed a strong relationship with my brilliant editor there, Charles Harmon. Together we developed the idea of launching an ARCA art crime book series under the auspices of Rowman & Littlefield, the largest independent publisher in the United States. The book you hold now began in an older form as part of that small-scale Kickstarter campaign and is now a new, expanded, updated volume that is among the first to be published as part of this series. The goal is to bring the best scholarship on art crime to a single series within one excellent publishing house, establishing what is the first publishing series in the world dedicated to this fascinating, understudied topic.

The book you hold now is an essay collection primarily drawn from my journalism on art crime. Most of the essays here were first published in major newspapers and magazines, including the *Guardian* and the *Washington Post*, and they were written from 2012 or so to the present. It is a book without a single narrative running throughout, and therefore it can be read piecemeal, each essay functioning as a standalone thought. But read the essays together and you'll come away with a strong, deep understanding of art crime—forgery, theft, security, looting in times of peace and war, art law and policy—based on a constellation of case studies. I have updated and rewritten essays, but have left in some time-linking elements (for instance, when I include an obituary of the artist Ulay, which was written the day after his death, I've kept "last night"). I hope that this will let the essays retain their freshness and immediacy. All the essays are on evergreen subjects—none is a hot take—and so reading them, even years later, is still entirely relevant in considering the case studies and the larger issues they bring to the fore.

Thank you for buying this book: a percentage of the profits go to ARCA's research and educational activities. To learn more about ARCA, you're welcome to visit www.artcrimeresearch.org. Thank you for your support, and happy reading!

—Dr. Noah Charney
Founder, ARCA

Acknowledgments

I would like to thank all of ARCA's staff, past and present, without whom the organization would never have taken off and endured. Particular thanks go to Lynda Albertson (our stalwart CEO), Urška Charney (our designer and my wife), Edgar Tijhuis (our academic director), and Crispin Corrado (our past academic director). For this series, warmest thanks go to Charles Harmon, my lovely editor at Rowman & Littlefield, without whom this series would not exist.

Some of the essays in this collection were first published, in most cases in a different form, elsewhere. This includes the *Guardian*, the *Art Newspaper*, *Salon*, the *Observer*, the *Washington Post*, the *Daily Beast*, and the *Journal of Art Crime*.

For more information on ARCA and its activities, please visit www.artcrimeresearch.org.

We encourage readers to consider applying as students to our annual postgraduate program, in which we have had students age twenty-one to eighty-two, from all over the world. You might also consider other books in our series or a subscription to the *Journal of Art Crime*, ARCA's twice-yearly, peer-reviewed academic journal, the first in the field.

Thank you for reading and for your support!

1 FRAUD AND FORGERY

Professor of Art Crime

If you stand before Rubens's majestic *Adoration of the Magi* in King's College Chapel, you will see a gorgeous painting, colossal in size and accomplishment. But you will not yet see its scars. In order to do so, you must maneuver over to either side of the painting, and view it in a raking light. If you do so, you will see that the canvas bears the remnant scars of three letters that were carved into it during the tumultuous 1970s. Those three letters are I-R-A.

The image of an art thief conjures prowling cat burglars and mustachioed villains cackling in cliff-top castles, surrounded by a museum of stolen paintings. This romanticized image has some roots in reality, but precious few. It comes from a handful of pre–World War Two art thefts that had the trappings of gentlemanliness. Individual, nonviolent thieves stealing art for ideological, as well as financial, reasons. These headline-making crimes captured the popular imagination and inspired best-selling fiction, stories of Raffles and Arsène Lupin loping along rooftops with sacks full of jewelry and hot art. Such stories, mingling fiction with truth too bizarre to be real, such as the "impossible" theft of Leonardo's *Mona Lisa* from the Louvre in 1911, made art crime a sexy topic. It is too easy to forget that art crime is indeed a crime, and a serious one. In fact, few members of the public, and even few police, know the realities of this crime type, which are far darker than most imagine. Since World War Two, art crime has been largely the realm of organized crime, from local gangs to international syndicates. Because of this, a stolen painting might be used as barter or collateral for other illicit goods, like drugs and arms. The US Department of Justice ranked art crime as the third-highest-grossing criminal trade worldwide, after only drugs and arms, and the UK Threat Assessment has noted its link to organized crime and even terrorism, from the IRA to Al-Qaeda. Illicit trade in looted antiquities is a known funding source for terrorist groups. Prior to September 11, terrorist Mohammed Atta tried to sell looted Afghani antiquities in

Germany in order to buy a plane to use in the 2001 attacks. Hijacking planes had been Plan B.

I came to study art crime through art history. Having grown up in the United States (New Haven, the Yale college town), I had always idealized British universities, and for whatever reason Cambridge was the place I sought to study, without ever giving real thought to Oxford. I studied art history at Colby College, in Maine in the United States, a very good, very small liberal arts undergraduate institution. I applied to a master's program at the Courtauld Institute and directly to a PhD at Cambridge—I'm not sure what I was thinking, most likely I wasn't thinking particularly clearly about the process. I just knew that my fantasy was to study at Cambridge. To my shock I was accepted at both institutions. I'm guessing that this had more to do with very kind recommendations than my grades, which were fine but not particularly exciting. I was geared up to go to Cambridge, directly into a PhD, when my art history professors at Colby made two suggestions.

First, they noted that I really had no preparation for a PhD. Even my honors thesis at Colby did not require the sort of independent, in-depth research that a British postgraduate degree would require. British students would have had three years or more of undergraduate study in their subject of choice, whereas I, as a liberal arts student, had taken only 50 percent of my college classes in art history, with the rest given over to whims and interests, from ancient Greek (which did not catch on) to a hands-on seminar in furniture making. The US PhD system is a very different creature. It takes about seven years, for starters, and students begin taking classes, then teach, and only then, several years in, begin their thesis. In Cambridge, art history PhDs require no classes, no requirement to teach—you simply have three years to research and write your thesis, largely on your own in terms of motivation. Professors advise but do not corral students into doing their work (as they tend to in the United States). So I just might be getting ahead of myself, to jump at age twenty-two into a Cambridge PhD. I think they probably thought that there had been a clerical error, something I wondered too, in my direct acceptance to a PhD without having a master's under my belt.

Their second point was that, as an art historian, I'd be crazy not to go to Courtauld. The Courtauld Institute is still the single best place to go to study art history (the year I attended I believe it was number one, and Cambridge was number three in the United Kingdom). It is one of the few places that still teaches connoisseurship, the intrinsic knowledge of an artist or period that has largely been supplanted by provenance research and forensics in order to authenticate works. In retrospect I am really pleased that I took the advice of my professors. I finished an MA in text and image in seventeenth-century

Roman art and architecture at Courtauld, deferring my entrance to Cambridge. I then went to Cambridge, thrilled to be accepted at St. John's College, and completed a second MA (the Cambridge MPhil) in art history, writing on Bronzino's London *Allegory of Love and Lust*, long my favorite painting.

It was during my year at the Courtauld Institute that I wrote my first novel. I had been an aspiring playwright, and had even acquired an agent in London to represent my plays. But that agent also said that, to really make a career as an author, the best way forward was to write fiction. Did I have a novel? Yes, I replied, and then frantically wrote what would become my first novel, *The Art Thief* (2007). I was incredibly fortunate that this became an international bestseller and allowed me to begin a career as a full-time writer.

Research for this novel is what led me from art history to study art crime. I had worked at Christie's, in Boston and London, and had worked at the Yale British Art Center, that wonderful museum in New Haven that, thanks to the generosity of Paul Mellon, has the second-largest collection of British art in the world, behind the Tate. I knew how the art world worked from behind the scenes and saw it as a world that the general public finds intriguing but knows relatively little about. I thought that it would make an ideal setting for a novel, a mystery or a thriller. So I set about researching art theft. This was shortly after *The Da Vinci Code* and *The Thomas Crown Affair*, and it was with these in mind that I prepared my own novel. It would incorporate art theft, forgery, smuggling, and museum security, but it should also be as realistic as possible. Plot mechanisms, and the action sequences in particular, should be plausible, and the fiction could therefore act as a vehicle to introduce art crime and art history to readers in a painless way.

While researching I realized that relatively little had been written about art crime. There were perhaps one hundred books, most out of print, and most journalistic accounts that did not place the crimes in a historical, international, or theoretical context. The stories were certainly intriguing, and I found that everyone from professors to cab drivers wanted to learn more about art crime. But there was a gap in the scholarship. This, I would later learn, was due to the field of art crime straddling several disciplines (art history, archaeology, criminology, security studies, policing, art law, museum studies). It therefore required a willingness on the part of the student to delve into subjects outside of one's area of expertise, which is not really the done thing in academia. An art historian would be discouraged from dipping into criminology, just as an archaeologist would find it intimidating to study art law. But art crime is inherently interdisciplinary—it is the study of crimes involving objects and victims. The objects have a rich history and a value that is largely nonintrinsic (a painting is canvas and pigment, its value derived from its story and the way its ingredients are used, rather than jewelry, for instance, the value of which is largely intrinsic, precious metals and gems). I determined to approach art crime from a variety of disciplines. Trained in art history, I was most interested in the story behind the artwork, its physical history as an object, why it was desired, why it was considered important, and—in some cases—worth killing or dying for. I already knew about the strange organism that is the art world. The art trade still runs to a certain extent on eighteenth-century standards, adhering to a gentleman's code of anonymity that derived from the dissolution of aristocratic art collections when the families could no longer afford to keep them but did not want to advertise their straitened circumstances. Christie's and Sotheby's would therefore sell a lot as "property of a gentleman" or "property of a lady," and leave it at that. Handshakes were considered acceptable, cash paid for wildly expensive objects, and objects as pricy as houses traded without a consistent chain of documentation (provenance) proving ownership and the legitimacy of the object in question. Unscrupulous individuals find many a shadow in which to lurk within the art world and, more specifically, the art trade. Con men, forgers, thieves, and tomb raiders can take advantage of the unusual, veiled art world. This was a murky world that I could already navigate, and which I would explore as deeply as I could.

I switched from art history to the history department at Cambridge and began a PhD in the history of art theft. I taught myself the criminology, law, archaeology, the policing, the security techniques. I got one year into my PhD, still frankly more interested in the popular stories than the raw academia, when I organized a conference at Cambridge, with the assistance of the Centre for Research in the Arts, Social Sciences and Humanities (CRASSH). The conference brought together leading art investigators and professors from among the relatively small group of international figures who study and investigate art crime. I had stumbled on a niche that boasted perhaps a few dozen figures worldwide who had also focused on the subject. Representatives from Scotland Yard, the FBI, the Carabinieri, the Tate museums, the Hong Kong police, and many more attended. Though I had not realized it at the time, this 2006 conference was the first to bring together academics and police to study this phenomenon, and it attracted the international media. A journalist in attendance wrote a feature article in the *New York Times Magazine* about the conference and about my work as a student of this "new" field, the study of art crime. This coincided with the release of my novel, *The Art Thief*. I was suddenly a (very) minor celebrity, and I had barely finished a year of my PhD.

It is difficult to put into words what being featured in the *New York Times* does to one's life. As it is read by millions (around seventeen million back then) it suddenly opens up worlds that marketing agencies literally could not buy. I was barraged with requests from television producers to develop an art crime drama series, an art crime documentary series that I would host, a feature film; agents asked if I was represented, if they might help to publish my PhD when I finished it. One media story bred others, around the world, from China to Chile, and I did dozens of interviews. This was coupled with the publicity orchestrated by the publisher of *The Art Thief*, and the result was quite a storm—all very good for a career as a writer, but not so good for a relatively young student struggling with a PhD in the history department of the University of Cambridge. I recognized that I was not focused enough on my PhD, and my kindly advisor did as well. I essentially had to make a choice: clamp down and focus on the PhD, or give it up and embrace this promising career as a writer, riding the media wave. My decision was aided by the fact that I had the option to go on an extensive book tour, a rarity these days as it is very expensive for publishers. I went with what seemed to me the surest career path, and the one that I would most enjoy. I thanked my advisor and, with not a little regret, dropped out of Cambridge to embark on a book tour that would take me to twelve cities in fourteen days. I would later complete a PhD in architectural history at University of Ljubljana, in Slovenia (where my wife is from), but that was the end of my Cambridge sojourn.

It was not the end of my involvement with the academic side of art crime, however. Inspired by the enthusiasm of the participants in the Cambridge conference, I founded a not-for-profit research group to promote the study of art crime. ARCA, the Association for Research into Crimes against Art, began with a core of trustees who had spoken at the CRASSH conference in 2006. Several years later, and ARCA is now the established go-to source for many members of the media, investigators, and students of art crime. ARCA, based in the United States and in Italy, runs a postgraduate certificate program every summer in Italy, the only program in the world that allows for the interdisciplinary study of art crime (also featured in the *New York Times*). ARCA has also published books (*Art and Crime: Exploring the Dark Side of the Art World* and *Art Crime: Terrorists, Tomb Raiders, Forgers and Thieves*) and releases a twice-yearly, peer-reviewed academic journal, *Journal of Art Crime* (many of the essays in this book first appeared there in a different form). We give annual awards to prominent professionals in our field, lecture broadly, and host an annual conference, a continuation of the CRASSH event, that is held in Umbria. I've been teaching art crime ever since.

I write both fiction and nonfiction, and my last twenty-plus books have all been nonfiction. I also work as a broadcaster, presenting on television and radio (including for the BBC), hosting podcasts, leading influencer campaigns (for Samsung, among others), and teaching online courses (for Yale University,

Atlas Obscura, the Smithsonian, and the National Gallery UK). The goal of this multimedia career is to introduce the facts about art history and art crime through engaging stories to the widest possible audience.

My hope is that readers and viewers will be drawn to art crime and art history for the great stories behind the history, whether told through informed fiction or engaging nonfiction. But once there, they will learn the truths about art crime, that it is not just the art that is at stake but a lot more, considering the involvement of organized crime and terrorist groups. From the IRA activist who slashed Rubens's *Adoration of the Magi* at King's College Chapel to the Taliban's demolition of the Bamiyan Buddhas and Mohammed Atta's attempts to attack the World Trade Center with a plane purchased with looted antiquities, there are far darker aspects of the protection and recovery of art that are important to keep in mind. Thomas Crown has roots in Victorian and Edwardian art heists, but the idea of the gentleman art thief is largely the construct of overenthusiastic journalists and fiction writers. Art crime is very serious indeed. The next time you visit a gallery, a rural church, an Etruscan archaeological site, or even see a painting hanging on the wall of a friend's home, consider that there is far more at stake should art disappear than the world seems to realize.

Art in the Age of Digital Reproduction

You enter the cave. The walkway you traverse winds around spot-lit, saber-toothed stalactites and stalagmites, and the rough-skin texture of the stone walls, slick in the perpetual dark damp. Your flashlight picks out first one, then more, of the prehistoric paintings on the wall. A deer, bison, a rhinoceros, painted onto the wall in charcoal black by hands that were protohuman. We are in the Chauvet cave, thirty-five thousand years old. Or are we? Something is missing. Even the blind could tell that. The scent is all wrong. Instead of damp and darkness, it smells of, well, tourists. For we are not in the Chauvet cave itself, which is closed to the public, since the atmospheric conditions which preserve the fragile paintings inside must be maintained. No, we are in the Caverne du Pont d'Arc, a just-opened replica of the Chauvet cave, accurate down to the last undulation of the stone wall, to the last stalactite (with an added catwalk and lighting, of course), but patently false.

Now travel, blindfolded, to some anonymous, freshly built art museum. Down goes the blindfold, and you stand before Van Gogh's *Almond Blossoms*. Surely you must be in the Van Gogh Museum in Amsterdam, you think. Why, it's obviously a Van Gogh, with his globular, three-dimensional application of vast, snotty quantities of oil, so much so that his paint casts a shadow. But no. You're looking at a work from the Relievo collection, an odd package offered (for a quarter million) by the Van Gogh Museum itself to extremely wealthy collectors and institutions that would quite like nine of the Van Gogh Museum's greatest-hit paintings on their walls but cannot get them, thanks to the inconvenience of most art being unique (and prohibitively expensive). These reproductions are pinpoint accurate as they are made with sophisticated three-dimensional scanning and three-dimensional printing, so every brushstroke is just as Van Gogh made it. Only Van Gogh did not make it. A printer did.

Welcome to what we might call "art in the age of digital reproduction." We are riffing on the famous essay by Walter Benjamin entitled "Art in the Age of Mechanical Reproduction," which argued that great, and authentic, artworks have a certain, undefinable "aura" about them that makes them great. Reproductions, whether mechanical (as they were when Benjamin was writing) or digital (in our own era) are missing this. We might even risk calling this the "soul" of the work. But it is a key component that art lovers find missing when they see a digital copy.

I specify digital copy, because that is very different from a forgery. In my book *The Art of Forgery* (2015), I discuss whether a forgery of a great work of art can, itself, be a great work of art. After all, most forgeries that make any headway in fooling experts are unique works themselves, made by hand by an artist in fraudulent imitation of the work of some other, more famous artist. Those are "originals," in that they are created by a passionate craftsman. They are just made in a derivative style and then later passed off as something they are not. Such unique, handmade forgeries, created with skill and ardor, can indeed be great works of art unto themselves, although in the same vein as those by assistants in a master's studio. With few exceptions, the past few millennia of master artists worked in the studio system. The master was the head of a studio, consisting of apprentices (who functioned like live-in interns) and paid assistants. All the works that emerged from the studio were under the authorship of the master, Rembrandt, for example, who was licensed by the local painter's guild to run the studio and accept commissions. But the paintings would have been created by a team: designed by the master, supervised by the master, with the master adding the finishing touches, with much of the actual painting, especially underlayers, still lifes, architectural features, backgrounds, clothing, and so on, handled by apprentices and assistants. The mark of a good assistant was his ability to paint in a way indistinguishable from the master's style, so that the works emerging from this studio would appear to have been created by a single artist. This has almost always been the way, with the few artists who did not run studios (Caravaggio, for example) the exceptions rather than the rule. Depending on how much you paid a master, you might get a work entirely painted by Rembrandt, and pay a fortune, or a work simply designed by Rembrandt but painted entirely by his staff, for a much more modest sum. This does not mean that the less expensive option is "bad," and it is still technically called a "Rembrandt" (as I discussed in the BBC documentary called *The Banker's Guide to Art*). It is essentially an entirely legal, artist-sanctioned forgery.

But it is a different story altogether when we speak of scanned and printed works of art, copies that were made only by computers and mechanisms, never by a human hand. And they do not have to be copies of existing works. The Next Rembrandt project saw scientists develop a brand-new painting of a brand-new subject and composition, but in the style of Rembrandt, digitally designed and printed to look like a lost work by the master. Aesthetically, and when viewed on a computer or television screen, it convinces. And since the most successful art forgers do not copy existing works, but create new works that they attempt to pass off as lost works by an established master, the compelling nature of this digital experiment is disturbing. It is when you see such a work in person that the veils can be peeled back. One can just "feel" the inauthenticity of the Caverne du Pont d'Arc cave paintings, of the Relievo van Goghs, of the "new" Rembrandt. These digital copies lack Benjamin's aura. That aura is what divides the real world from the Matrix. Connoisseurship, an innate feeling for art and authenticity, is the Through-the-Looking-Glass pill that allows some experts, and some passionate amateurs, to feel the difference between art that emerged from a three-dimensional human hand, versus a three-dimensional printer.

The danger is that the less-passionate amateurs and so-called "experts" might not be able to tell the difference at all. Or, worse, they might see the digital copy and decide that it is not worth the effort to see the original. Those are the folks who choose to stay plugged into the Matrix. Not because it is better, but because it is easier.

The Art World Wants to Be Deceived

There are three ways to authenticate art. The first, as mentioned, is a stylistic analysis, also called connoisseurship. Connoisseurship used to be the primary method of authenticating art. An expert would develop an intrinsic familiarity with an artist's oeuvres through seeing and studying every one of their extant works. The ability to recognize an artist's hand was used to determine the authenticity of newly discovered works purported to be by that artist, as they came on the market. Connoisseurs are decidedly unscientific, indeed, often dismissing science as merely the default authentication method for those insufficiently knowledgeable. Experts took obvious pleasure in their ability to recognize authenticity, which they often claimed was unique, preternatural. A British slang term for connoisseurs was "divvies," as in those capable of "divining" the authenticity of mysterious works through their personal communion with them. Connoisseurship is a bit of a dinosaur these days, a parlor trick, taught only at the Courtauld Institute in London, the world's premiere art history school (full disclosure: I studied at the Courtauld and was taught connoisseurship, which I still thoroughly admire as a method). Science and provenance research have superseded it as the main tool of authentication. And yet the mystique of the connoisseur, and a preference to rely on the word of an expert (be they fakes or authentic experts themselves), still pervades the art world today. And millions of dollars, as well as professional reputations, still ride on the word of these pseudo-mystics.

Experts will examine brushstroke, application and thickness of paint, the way artists painted certain recurring themes (Vermeer's pearls were painted with exactly one stroke), the content of the work (did Caravaggio ever paint a deposition?), and a more evasive "feeling" that one gets from a work. The example frequently mentioned is that connoisseurs recognize an authentic work the way you might recognize a friend of yours in the middle of a crowded square. You just know.

This doesn't sound very scientific, and it isn't. However, this was the preferred method of authentication for centuries, until the twentieth century. But one of the problems with so-called art expertise is that there has never been a national or international standard that determines who can be called an expert. There is no equivalent, for example, of medical school standards or of the bar exam. Some "experts" have never even studied art formally. It was only in the mid-nineteenth century, with its development in German universities, that one could study art history in an academic setting. Art expertise was generally passed down from artist to pupil, from collector to inheritor, and only later from professor to art history student. Not only could anyone be an expert, but anyone could dole out the invaluable certificates of authenticity, papers that accompanied an artwork and assured the potential buyer of its legitimacy. Whether the provider of the certificate was, in fact, truly an expert was less important than having the certificate to accompany the work. Certain very famous experts could guarantee a lucrative sale if they provided a certificate. Most famous perhaps was Bernard Berenson, who worked with the great dealer Joseph Duveen.

Their relationship was marked with a waft of conflict of interest—for Berenson was paid a commission, a percentage of the sale price of each artwork he authenticated. It was, therefore, in Berenson's interest to find each work to be as rare and valuable as possible. The better method, though not without problems, was to set a fee paid to an expert for a certificate, regardless of the value of the work and regardless of the outcome of the certification (which might deem a work inauthentic or by a different artist).

Scientific Analysis

The scientific analysis of art to prove authenticity is a new phenomenon, and one of its pioneers, whose story is detailed in *A Real Van Gogh* by Henk Tromp, was Maarten de Wilde. His use of pigment analysis, incorporating chemistry techniques to determine the composition of paints in questionable paintings, then comparing them to the composition of paints in confirmed authentic works, led to the dismissal of a very expensive "Van Gogh" owned by the renowned American collector Chester Dale, when his painting was found to contain resin—an agent that sped the oil paint's drying, and which Van Gogh never used. A forger had used it to make the fresh oil look decades old. Such analyses are now a preferred method, considered surer and certainly more objective than personal expertise, the word of one so-called expert versus another. Conservation is a science, one heavily involved with chemistry, so it is only a small step to enlist the aid of chemists in issues of authentication. The art world, however, has been resistant to the breakup of the established mystical order of connoisseurs. The other problem with science is that it is not as easy to debate. When one expert claims your painting is inauthentic, you can always choose to ignore that expert and search for another who believes the work is the real deal (or who will say that he does for the right price). Science offers less leeway. Scientific analysis can also be expensive, and sometimes destructive (carbon dating, for instance, requires the destruction of a tiny portion of a work in order to provide its date). But the larger problem is that while science may be more objective, it often determines more "maybes" than definitive answers. For instance, in the case of a Van Gogh, it was determined that the work had been painted within the last forty years—which, at the time, meant that it could have been painted by Van Gogh toward the end of his life, or that it might have been painted twenty years after he died. Our postmodern era tendency is to assume that science will answer all questions. But many forgers come from a background in conservation and therefore know the tests that their forgeries will need to overcome. There are examples of fake ancient Chinese pottery which forgers injected with a radioactive isotope at the probable location that a conservator would choose for a test sample, so that carbon dating would be fooled. And the blinding light of science can be used by shady characters in shining armor, as the 2010 *New Yorker* article about the authenticator and suspected forger Peter Paul Biro made clear.

Provenance

The last two decades have seen a rise in the art world's reliance on provenance, the documented history of an object (usually an ownership history), to assure themselves of a work's legitimacy, both as an authentic work and as a work that was not stolen or looted. The problem with provenance, however, is that it relies on historical documents that rarely survive intact over the centuries. Could you locate the receipt from the last mattress you bought? If not, try to imagine someone keeping track of receipts of sale dating back five hundred years, when a painting or piece of furniture was first made. It is very unusual to find provenance that is complete and intact. And with the inevitable gaps, and the not uncommon phenomenon of a legitimate work having no provenance to speak of, the system is still a porous one. There are also examples of forgers using the reliance on provenance to their advantage. John Myatt and John Drewe created false documents to act as provenance for the forged paintings they created and then inserted them into real archives, so that diligent researchers would "discover" them and link them to the forged paintings.

In the end, some combination of scientific analysis and provenance provides the strongest argument for authenticity. But there are ways to beat any system, and the art world still relies to an astonishing degree on expertise, which is still unregulated. By talking the talk, saying what the art trade wants to hear, anyone can claim to be an expert and so establish a career.

Counterfeit Money

While counterfeit money is its own field of study, it has many parallels with art forgery, and we therefore have seen fit to consider it in this chapter. In doing so, I thought that it might be of interest to present a brief history of counterfeit money, for those unfamiliar with the subject. Perhaps the most well-known sort of forgery is the faking of money, whether counterfeiting coins, dollar bills, or treasury bonds. The United States Secret Service, before they became best known as the bodyguards of the president, was established in order to investigate counterfeit money printing operations and close them down.

Counterfeit money is any money produced, even at an official mint, that is not officially sanctioned. One can see why it is important to regulate the amount of money in circulation. Too much results in inflation, which can ruin an economy. The Nazis forged British pounds and American dollars during the Second World War, in an effort to flood their enemy's economy, as did the British during the Revolutionary War—they produced Continental dollars in order to overwhelm the nascent American economy.

Money is also an odd subject because, through it, we assign value to something that is traded instead of an object of actual value, as would be the case in a barter system. Pieces of paper are used instead of having to carry objects to trade, from pigs to precious metals. The assignment of value that is nonintrinsic (because paper money, at least, is not made of precious materials) to a tradable commodity is akin to our discussions of art: for paintings on canvas, for example, the value of the object is nonintrinsic.

As in the case of art, we must rely on the sustained value of those pieces of paper we call money. In 2011, debates raged in the United States about whether we should revert to a gold standard—a quantity of gold kept in vaults that would equal every piece of paper money in circulation and which, in theory, every citizen could swap their paper money for, if they so choose. Whether there is a gold or silver standard, or any standard at all, is also a bit odd: Who was the first person to determine that gold or silver should be treasured, and more universally accepted as currency than paper money, or indeed pigs? The ancient Celts used to carry their money on their bodies, wearing rings of gold around their necks. It seems that gold has always been considered precious, and so it has history on its side, to justify itself as an international default to currency. But it still can feel arbitrary, that a nugget of gold should be prized and a nugget of pyrite (fool's gold), which looks the same to the untrained eye, should be of little value.

Faking money has a rich history and is a big business. It seems logical that counterfeiting would have begun shortly after the introduction of money, and examples of forged coins have been found dating back to ancient Rome. Roman coins were minted, rather than made from molds, so the discovery at archaeological sites of molds of Roman coins means that the coins created from them would have been counterfeit.

Fear over counterfeit money has influenced the way that money is produced. The milled or reeded edges of coins (think of a US quarter, with its grooves carved onto the edge) are both a blind aid, to identify which coin you are feeling in a purse or a pocket, and are also meant to demonstrate that the metal of which the coin is made is not merely present on the outside of the coin, a thin skin. Dollar bills are incredibly detailed, including watermarks, holograms, raised intaglio printing (that you can feel with your finger), and are woven through with miniscule wires, all of which are meant to make them all but impossible to reproduce in a manner that will fool testing.

The earliest known use of coins dates to circa 600 BC, where coinage began in the Greek city of Lydia. The earliest counterfeit technique was to coat a less-valuable metal coin in a thin layer of the more precious metal (usually gold or silver), resulting in what is called a "fourrée." Our modern legacy of grooved edges to coins is a direct descendant of attempts to prove that the official coins in circulation are not fourrées.

The art of counterfeit detection can be dated to at least 80 BC, when Cicero wrote of an M. Marius Gratidianus, a praetor who was praised for developing a test to detect counterfeit Roman denarii coins and removing fakes from circulation. Ironically, Gratidianus was executed under the reign of Sulla, who introduced what is perhaps the earliest antiforgery law. The Lex Cornelia de Falsis made official the practice of making coins with grooved edges. Denarii coins were produced with around twenty notches chiseled around the edge. But the discovery of notched fourrée denarii shows that the measure was not wholly successful. The best way to identify a fake coin, like a fourrée, is by weight—a solid gold coin will have a different weight than a fourrée coin, coated in gold but largely of a less valuable metal, such as copper.

There are far too many examples of money counterfeiters to fit in our history, but a few examples through history will give a sense of the field. Counterfeiting has long been considered a crime likened to treason, with similarly capital punishments meted out. In China, early paper money was produced from mulberry trees. Mulberry forests were therefore heavily guarded, and counterfeiters executed. In 1690, Thomas and Anne Rogers were dramatically executed for having faked forty pieces of silver. "King" David Hartley, an infamous counterfeiter in the eighteenth century, was hanged in 1770. Because counterfeiting could severely damage a nation's economy, the crime of forging money was considered an attack against the state.

Benjamin Franklin himself said "to counterfeit is death," recognizing the importance to a nation that its currency be reliable. British counterfeiters creating fake Continental dollars during the American Revolutionary War were called "shovers," as they forcibly inserted fake currency into the American market. Two infamous "shovers," John Blair and David Farnsworth, were captured with ten thousand fake Continental dollars. They were tortured, at George Washington's insistence, to extract information about the British counterfeiting operation, before they were executed. But, every now and then, a master counterfeiter was put to use, rather than to the sword: a barber called Alexander, who forged coins in Byzantium during the reign of Emperor Justinian, was caught and then employed by the empire to ferret out other counterfeiters (much as forgers John Myatt and Tom Keating assisted police in investigating at-large art forgers). And while the Union, during the American Civil War, tried to flood the Confederacy with fake Confederate currency, their fake money turned out to be of better quality than the originals that the Confederacy was producing and was therefore more valuable.

Modern technology, particularly the use of computers and software like Photoshop, has made it easier to produce relatively unconvincing counterfeit currency, but also permits what are called "superdollars"—currency that is of the highest quality and can even fool scientific tests that seek to distinguish fake currency from authentic. Estimates through the 2000s suggested that an average of $1 to $3 out of every $10,000 used were counterfeits that would not fool someone if closely examined, while only about $3 out of every $100,000 were counterfeits that were difficult to detect.

Counterfeiting is an extremely big business today, and the United States Secret Service has its hands full keeping tabs on it. A 2010 study on the volume of fake US currency in circulation worldwide estimates that one or fewer counterfeit notes is in circulation for every ten thousand genuine notes. While that may seem like a small number, if it is multiplied by ten thousand, it means that for every legitimate $100 million, there are $10,000 in fakes. The 2010 GDP (gross domestic product) of the state of Texas alone was $1.936 billion. That means that for the GDP of one state, there is around $1.93 million in counterfeit money circulating.

David Bowie: Artist Forger

On April Fools' Day, 1998, the crème de la crème of the New York art scene gathered for a party in the studio of Jeff Koons. David Bowie played host, and while a who's who of the art crowd mingled over canapes and cocktails, the mastermind behind what would be (perhaps overzealously) dubbed "the biggest art hoax in history" prowled the perimeters of the party. It was the key event to launch an elaborate practical joke concocted by Bowie and his friend, the Scottish novelist William Boyd, multi-award-winning author of numerous novels, most famously *Any Human Heart*. Bowie and Boyd met while both were members of the editorial board for *Modern Painters* magazine and quickly hit it off. Both were outsiders in the sense that they were art lovers but not involved in the art world directly, as a rock star and a star novelist. After a meeting in 1998, they bounced the idea around of introducing a fictitious artist into the magazine. Rolling with this idea, Boyd developed a fictitious history of a "lost American artist" by the name of Nat Tate.

With a novelist's flair, Boyd developed a complete backstory for Tate: An orphan born in New Jersey in 1928, adopted by a family on Long Island, sent to art school, and established in Greenwich Village in the 1950s. Tate met Picasso and Braque in France, but this triggered self-doubt, rather than inspiration. Returning to New York, Tate burned most of his oeuvre. Substance abuse and depression led to his suicide on January 12, 1960, aged only thirty-one. It was a dramatic tale but one in touch with the history of art, which is unfortunately full of tragic stories of early deaths, from Giorgione and Raphael to Basquiat and beyond. It also conveniently allowed for the lack of documentation about the life of Tate, as well as the paucity of surviving works. But coming up with the story was the easy part. Building physical evidence to back the story proved much trickier.

In an issue of the *Journal of Art Crime*, an article by Charlotte Rebecca Britton entitled "Forging a Double Life: Creating an Artist for the Purpose of Fraud" looked at an unusual phenomenon: "an artist being created for the purpose of promoting counterfeit art." This is such an elaborate con that it has rarely been practiced, but her article (particularly impressive when one considers that she had only recently graduated from the ARCA Postgraduate Program in Art Crime and Cultural Heritage Protection) cites several examples, one of them involving a hugely prominent name, and yet the case is strangely little known.

To really make the story believable, Bowie and Boyd decided to publish a lavish monograph about the artist. Going with a publisher in Germany made it trickier for the anglophone public to ask questions. The friends reveled in the details, filling the book with plausible-looking footnotes, selecting historical photographs that they captioned as being of Nat Tate and his circle. Boyd, an amateur artist, even created some pieces to be featured in the catalogue as the work of Nat Tate. Bowie and Boyd recruited some celebrity colleagues who were in on the joke to offer bona fides and blurbs for the book cover, including Gore Vidal and Picasso's biographer, John Richardson. Bowie included a quote, as well, stating: "The great sadness of this quiet and moving monograph is that the artist's most profound dread—that God will make you an artist but only a mediocre artist—did not in retrospect apply to Nat Tate."

The April Fools' Day party in 1998 was officially the launch of *Nat Tate: An American Artist, 1928–1960*, released as the first book from Bowie's own publishing house, 21. Bowie read excerpts from the book and a British journalist, David Lister—who was also in on the joke—moved among the guests and instigated discussions about Tate, predicating his comments on the assumption that the partygoers had heard of Tate prior to that night. Apparently, some of them had—a few guests could even recall having attended Tate's exhibits in New York in the 1950s. Such is the power of suggestion.

This event was considered such a success that a London book release party was scheduled for the following week, but Lister was a bit too delighted with the proceedings. He broke the story of the hoax in the *Independent* before the London art scene could have the wool pulled over its eyes.

This story of a "forged artist" is not one suited to the history of crime, as no crime was committed. No one was defrauded out of anything—no one lost money. It was an elaborate practical joke, but one which Boyd felt made a good point about the naïveté of the art world. "It's a little fable," he wrote, "particularly relevant now, when almost overnight, people are becoming art celebrities." The only kink in the scheme was Lister's article, as Boyd and Bowie intended the hoax to be drawn out, perhaps with an exhibit of Tate's remaining oeuvre at a major museum, and only to be revealed further down the line.

In Britton's essay, she notes that the Nat Tate practical joke provides a useful roadmap for how some of the criminal artist forgers went about falsifying our impressions of history in order to profit. Appropriating quotes from celebrated figures gives the impression of veracity—if someone like John Richardson, the leading authority on Picasso, says that Tate was a great artist, there is much peer pressure to agree. Seeing is believing, and the inclusion of photographs and actual works of art (whether they actually have anything to do with the subject) help reassure readers, as do the presence of footnotes—which no one bothers to check to see if a) they actually refer to real publications, or b) they do refer to real publications, whether the referenced sources have anything to do with the subject at hand. Referencing evidence seems to be enough to satisfy almost everyone, as few bother to check the evidence referenced, to see if it is actually connected to the story at hand.

While Boyd and Bowie did not seek profit from their hoax, it did catapult Boyd from a well-considered, award-winning novelist into the status of talk show celebrity. And while they did not intend to make money on the works in question, an auction at Sotheby's London in November 2011 sold a "rare surviving drawing from Tate's Bridge Series, *Bridge no. 114*, which was bought for 7250 pounds." The profits went to a charity.

Did Jeff Really Paint That Koons? Inside the Studio System

Word filtered down through the art community that superstar Jeff Koons, who along with Damien Hirst is the highest-earning artist in art history, laid off much of his staff. To be precise, in a series of downsizing moves, he fired some thirty members of his painting staff, which at one time numbered one hundred. This is the third round of layoffs since 2015. Most of those painters were brought on to work the "Gazing Ball" series, in which they hand-copied thirty-five Old Master paintings, to which a shiny, metallic-colored sphere was added. The layoffs occurred after the completion of this painting-heavy project.

There were grumblings of being vastly underpaid (Artnet reported that some were earning just $21 per hour, while Koons's works fetch millions at auction).

But what surprises many is not that Koons would so underpay the people actually creating his works, nor that he would downsize his staff, but rather there is confusion over how an artist produces works that are labeled as his own, when he may not actually have any hand in their making. Much was made of Damien Hirst's recent series of paintings, because he had actually painted them all himself. This may indeed sound like an odd statement. Don't all artists create their own works, you may ask.

This is actually part of a long art historical tradition, and it is not in the least unusual or surprising. We have the Romantic era, with a dose of Giorgio Vasari's 1550 group biography, *Lives of the Most Eminent Painters, Sculptors and Architects*, to thank for the general misconception that major, professional artists create their works alone. The idea of the lone, brooding artist, possibly depressed and drinking absinthe in a Parisian garret while wearing a black beret and chain-smoking, is actually the oddity. Most professional artists through history ran studios, often called bodegas.

To understand how studios work (and worked), we might look at a Renaissance master, or we might look to one of the most popular painters in the world, though nary a critic would raise their eyes to give him the time of day, Thomas Kincaide. The "Painter of Light," as he is sometimes called, employs an army of staff to paint his mildly cheesy, homey landscapes, the artistic equivalent of the Saturday afternoon made-for-TV Christmas films on Lifetime. Depending on how much you pay, you could get a work entirely hand-painted by Kincaide, for a small fortune, or for very little money you can get a work designed by the main man but painted entirely by staff. For even less money, you can buy a print of one of his paintings, touched up with hand-painted "highlights." There was a sliding scale of options to choose from, depending on how directly involved the master himself would be in your commission.

This is simply a continuation of the tradition of great Renaissance artists, like Domenico di Ghirlandaio. Commissioning a work by Ghirlandaio did not mean that the master would paint the work entirely himself, but rather that it was the product of his studio. The more one paid (or the more prestigious the patron), the more the master would work on the painting hands-on. In most cases, he would design it, supervise its painting, and likely handle the hands and faces, considered the two most difficult aspects to get right. But backgrounds, still-life elements, architecture, draperies, furniture, and the like would almost certainly be painted by paid assistants or indentured apprentices learning the trade. Since oil paint takes a long time to dry, and must be fairly dry before more layers can be applied, a studio might be working on many paintings at once, with panels tucked away to dry, while several might be propped up, to be actively worked on that day. Expensive pigments would be ground by hand and mixed according to proprietary recipes designed by the master—Ghirlandaio's preferred shade of yellow might differ from Michelangelo's or Bronzino's. The raw ingredients (panels, canvases, paints) would be prepared for painting by staff. The main difference between historical bodegas and contemporary studios is in the age and experience of the staff. Historical studios were part academies, part businesses. There would be paid assistants but also a team of apprentices, who were indentured to the master, housed and fed and trained, usually beginning age eight to twelve and apprentices until age sixteen to eighteen. At that point they could elect to remain in the employ of the master, now paid, move elsewhere, or submit their "masterpiece" to the local painters' guild. This was a single artwork entirely by their hand, by which the guild would determine whether they were skillful enough to be licensed to open their own studio.

Jeff Koons is best known for his monumental sculptures resembling balloon animals but made of glossy metal. But for most of his works, he might best be considered a conceptual artist, in that he conceives of the works, designs them, but rarely actually participates in their creation, on a hands-on basis. For this, he employs a vast staff, making him perhaps more like an architect than our traditional image of an artist. Architects concoct their creations, make designs for them, but contractors actually do the building. Koons and Hirst appear to be less involved in the actual creation than their Old Master counterparts were. They are the heads of corporations, making more money than the GNP of West Timor. Their studios lack the educational component of past masters and are built more like big businesses than local enterprises. Renaissance painters' guilds also rigorously controlled the total number of staff any studio could employ, in order to maintain quality. For example, in Rubens's Antwerp the maximum number of staff in a studio was fourteen (though Rubens skirted the law to exceed that number by a large margin). Koons, by contrast, employed around one hundred painters to create his "Gazing Ball" series but understandably no longer required so many when his projects tended to be sculptures. His reduction of staff was news mostly because of the low hourly fee he allegedly paid, and because of the general (mis)conception that most artists should paint most of their work themselves.

Giorgio Vasari's *Lives* (the subject of my 2017 book, *Collector of Lives: Giorgio Vasari and the Invention of Art*, coauthored with Ingrid Rowland), considered the first work of art history, is originally responsible for our idea that an artwork is the complete creative expression of a single mind and hand. Most of how we think about art and museums today has its origins in Vasari's hugely popular and influential group biography of Renaissance artists, many of whom he knew and worked with. By featuring masters of studios and weaving a cult around them, he downplayed the collaborative aspect of their work—this may have been a sort of defense mechanism, as he was sometimes accused of being lazy and relying too much on his own assistants. Then the Romantic era promoted the idea of lonely, forlorn, brooding artists struggling to make ends meet but producing powerful art at great personal sacrifice. This idea has melodramatic appeal, and it stuck in the popular imagination. While it has been true for many artists, particularly those in the modern era, before they make it big, the truly big-name artists, from ancient times to the present, have been more like architects or film directors, designing and supervising but not always getting their hands dirty.

How Do I Know It's Really a de Kooning?

TV shows, like *Container Wars* and *Storage Wars*, are dedicated to investors examining storage containers from a distance and offering serious cash, otherwise blind, to bid on ownership of the contents. Every once in a while, there is a jackpot, a eureka moment that turns a few thousand dollars into ten or even one hundred times that amount. Such was the case in 2018, when art dealer David Killen, who runs an eponymous gallery in New York, bid on a storage locker in New Jersey that had once been the property of an art conservator, Orrin Riley. Killen paid $15,000 for it, without thinking that much would come forth. The tradition is to require bidders for storage materials that have gone unclaimed to glance only passingly at the contents, so there is a large measure of gambling involved. You might end up with a treasure, but more often than not you're stuck with flea market junk. This locker did not look overly promising. In fact, according to Killen, an auction house had passed on the chance to buy its contents. But he figured, what the heck, he'd give it a shot. And what a shot it turned out to be.

Among an otherwise unremarkable jumble, there were some large boxes labeled "de Kooning." Inside were six lost paintings by one of the most prominent, and highest-selling, artists of the abstract expressionist movement in mid-twentieth-century New York. De Kooning paintings have sold for as much as $66.3 million. Here were six, not to mention what appeared to be a nice painting by Paul Klee. This was the sort of once in a lifetime moment that blind bidders can only dream of. In 2006, a painting by fellow abstract expressionist Jackson Pollock was bought at a thrift store for $5. It was later valued at $50 million. At a yard sale at a Louisiana trailer park, a woman bought what looked like a Picasso for $2. It was valued at $2 million but was handed over to the FBI, as it looked like a work registered as having been stolen. As recently as 1958, Leonardo's *Salvator Mundi*, thought then to be a nineteenth-century pastiche, sold for forty-five GBP. It is now the world's most expensive artwork, bought for $450.3 million. There are precedents for stumbling on lost masterpieces that can make your fortune. But how is it determined whether these de Koonings are really, well, de Koonings?

In this case, all evidence points to their authenticity, but shifting their value from the thousands into the millions requires a careful process.

Though found in a box labeled "de Kooning," they are not signed. That said, a signature is not really proof of anything, since signatures are among the least-reliable ways to authenticate an artwork—works were not regularly signed until the nineteenth century, and signatures can be far more easily forged than a whole artwork. Then where to turn to authenticate these paintings, and possibly transform a $15,000 storage locker into a bonanza worth tens of millions?

In the world of art authentication, there are three main categories to which hopeful owners may turn. The first is connoisseurship. The problem with this is that it is always a matter of opinion, even if that opinion is well educated. You can often find experts with equally impressive pedigrees who cannot agree on certain works. There is also the possibility of conflicts of interest, and clever forgers and confidence men have figured out ways to hoodwink even established experts. Consider, for example, the famous case of Han van Meegeren who, in the 1940s, forged paintings by Vermeer that did not look anything like any paintings anyone had ever seen by Vermeer, but which appeared to fulfill a hypothesis of a lost early period of Vermeer's work that Abraham Bredius, the world's leading Vermeer scholar, had theorized. It was a trap set by Van Meegeren for one man to fall into, but that one man happened to be the world's premiere Vermeer expert. When Bredius thought that he had found a painting that finally made plastic his controversial theory, he leaped upon it with enthusiasm and refused to back down from his estimation that not only was this a Vermeer, and not a forgery or derivative work, but it was one of the finest Vermeers he had ever seen. Experts can and do err with nerve-wracking frequency.

The other two categories for authentication are provenance research and forensic testing. Forensic testing is very good at spotting anachronisms that may appear in a work of art suggesting that it cannot be from the appropriate period (for instance, forger Wolfgang Beltracchi was caught when he used Titanium White paint in a work that predated the invention of that paint). However, forensics are very bad at indicating authorship, helping with the period in which a work was made, not with the hand that made it. Forensics, in the case of recent artworks like those by de Kooning, are not as useful. A work made in the 1950s or '60s would be easy to forge, in material terms, because it is easy to get canvas and paints from just a few decades ago. This means that scientific testing is unlikely to be particularly revelatory, aside from the hope that perhaps a de Kooning fingerprint might be found on the work, for example.

And so we turn to provenance research, which looks at the documented history of an object to see if there is a historical record of an object that could match the description of what has recently been found. This hopefully-a-de Kooning discovery is new enough that provenance research has not been made public. But the first stop would be to look at de Kooning's catalogue raisonné, which seeks to be the definitive encyclopedia of all of an artist's work, lost and accounted for. There might be references in a diary or a contract or a letter or an image in the background of a photograph that references these lost works and gives credence that they might be authentic, because they fit into the biography of the artist. In this case, the Willem de Kooning Foundation, which monitors the artist's legacy, does not offer an authentication service, so David Killen turned to the opinion of a connoisseur. He hired Lawrence Castagna, a specialist who knew de Kooning and his wife, and who is, theoretically, in as good a position as any to determine authenticity, based on the look and the vibe that these objects give off.

If that sounds rather unscientific, it's because it is. Art authentication is rarely an exact science, particularly in that almost mystical realm of connoisseurship, of one expert claiming to know their field so well that they could distinguish authorship simply by looking at something. More often than not, this is in fact the case, and experts prove their mettle. But they can also be fooled, as I chronicled with frequency in my book *The Art of Forgery*. However, my more recent book *The Museum of Lost Art* is the story of numerous works once lost but almost miraculously found again. So for every handful of questionable discoveries, like a lost "Michelangelo" crucifix that almost no experts thought was by Michelangelo, there are a few true rediscoveries of once-lost works, sometimes even masterpieces, which offer hope in situations such as this one.

Castagna has claimed that the paintings are, beyond doubt, by de Kooning. The story of the storage locker and its owners seems to fit well enough, in terms of potential provenance, to make this possible. So far, it looks as though David Killen has truly hit the jackpot. It almost makes me want to start watching TV shows about people bidding on storage containers. Almost . . .

On Alec Baldwin, Original Copies, and the Bait and Switch

In 2014, Matisse's *Odalisque in Red Trousers* was recovered, after an FBI sting operation, and returned to the Caracas Museum of Contemporary Art in Venezuela, from which it had been stolen in 2000—though it had never gone missing. At least, that's how it appeared. The real Matisse had been swiped back in 2002, but no one—no curator, no guard, no visitor, no staff member—had noticed, because the thieves had swapped a very good forgery in its place. It was only after two years, in 2002, that museum staff noticed that the switch had taken place. In retrospect, curators noted that the forgery was already in place in a September 2000 photograph of President Hugo Chávez, standing proudly in front of the museum's prized possession.

In August 1545, Duke Cosimo de' Medici of Florence requested that his court painter, Bronzino, paint a copy on panel of the *pala*, the centerpiece, of his frescoes in the chapel of Eleonora di Toledo in the Palazzo Vecchio, to be sent as a gift to a French diplomat who had just awarded Cosimo with the prestigious Order of the Golden Fleece.

Ely Sakhai, a respected art dealer with a swanky gallery in Manhattan, hatched a scheme to buy authentic paintings, have them secretly copied by Chinese forgers, and then sell the copies, with the provenance that had accompanied the originals. The real paintings stayed in his home. He would have gotten away with it, had he not grown hubristic (or some might say stupid) and tried to sell the original when, at the same time, a gallery that had bought the forgery tried to sell that—both in New York. Christie's and Sotheby's both had Gauguin's *Vase de Fleurs* in their May 2000 catalogues, Sotheby's with the original, Christie's with the forged version. They only noticed when the catalogues came out.

What do these stories have to do with Alec Baldwin?

More than you might think.

News broke this weekend of actor Alec Baldwin having been duped into buying a copy of a painting, *Sea and Mirror*, which he had long admired, when he thought he was buying the original. But it was an original that he bought—just not the original he had hoped for.

The first version of Ross Bleckner's *Sea and Mirror*, painted in 1996, sold at auction for $121,000 in 2007. For whatever reason, Baldwin fell in love with the painting but did not buy it then, instead carrying around a picture of it in his shoulder bag and quietly pining for the real thing. Fast-forward to 2010, when Baldwin asked art dealer Mary Boone, who represents Bleckner, if he might purchase *Sea and Mirror* then. Boone says that she told Baldwin that the owner wanted $175,000 to part with the painting, plus there would be $15,000 in gallery fees (her cut) for facilitating the transaction. For a man of Baldwin's wealth, this sounded like a good deal. Boone is said to have added, "Ross is so thrilled for you to have the painting and so am I."

Sea and Mirror was delivered to Baldwin's New York home, and he was so delighted that, at the 2012 Kennedy Center honors, the *New York Times* quoted him as saying, "I love this thing so much."

But Baldwin began to grow suspicious, even citing a new paint smell to this *Sea and Mirror* now hanging in his apartment. He called in an expert from Sotheby's, who confirmed his fears: this was not the original version he had fallen in love with. But it was also neither a fake nor a forgery.

Though in casual conversation the words are used interchangeably, the criminological definition of fakes and forgeries are distinct. A fake is an original work of art that is altered in some way to fraudulently pass it off as of greater value than it actually is. A forgery is a work made from scratch in fraudulent imitation of the work of another, more valuable artist. Baldwin's *Sea and Mirror* is neither—it is a copy by the original artist, and is therefore original.

So, what, then, is the fuss?

There are a number of reasons for fussing. But first, we should get one thing clear: there is a long history of artists copying their own works to satisfy the desires of clients. When a visiting diplomat admired Bronzino's paintings in the Palazzo Vecchio, Cosimo commissioned a copy to be sent as a gift. Leonardo da Vinci made two versions of his *Madonna of the Yarnwinder* (the Buccleuch version and the Lansdowne version) and may have made multiples of the *Mona Lisa* (those extant are thought to be by his studio, but the possibility remains). This practice was by no means limited to the Old Masters. Matisse made two versions of his famous *The Dance*; the 1909 version is on display at MoMA, the 1910 version at the Hermitage. Both are original, both by Matisse. In terms of historical and financial value, the first version of any work is considered the more important, but both are originals.

There have also been many bait and switches in the history of art collecting. *Art Market Monitor* reported a trial just opening in Singapore, in which a tour guide was entrusted by an eighty-nine-year-old widow with half a million dollars to buy a painting of a horse by artist Xu Beihong but instead brought her a replica, pocketing the (presumably very large) difference. There is no shortage of such cases, and it can happen even at the level of major museums and national cultural ministries. In 2007, the Hamburg Museum of Ethnology in Germany mounted a blockbuster exhibition of Terracotta Warriors, which were shipped over at great expense from China, only to realize, after ten thousand visitors had seen the exhibit, that they had been sent replicas. But there is a difference between replicas, original copies, and fakes or forgeries. In the Sakhai case, these were clearly forgeries—wholesale new works made with the intent to deceive. In the Caracas *Odalisque* case, an extremely good forgery was put in place to cover up the theft of the original. But Baldwin's case does not involve forgery, nor a replica (a copy made without the intent to deceive), but a bait and switch nonetheless, one involving two originals.

You can argue, of course, that Baldwin should have noticed that he had received the wrong painting much earlier. Even the untrained eye can tell that the two versions of *Sea and Mirror* are different. For someone who carried a copy of the picture in his shoulder bag for years, it is astonishing that he would not have noticed sooner. But such is the faith that collectors have in reputable dealers that such oversights, glaring in retrospect, can happen. The most famous recent case of this was with the now-defunct Knoedler Gallery, once Manhattan's oldest and most respected but recently tried for having knowingly sold forgeries, which their longtime clients accepted as authentic thanks to the gallery's bona fides (the case was settled before a verdict was reached, but the very fact of the settlement after a series of damning witnesses appeared to all as an admission of guilt).

What remains confusing is that the Manhattan district attorney, when approached by Baldwin, said that he could not bring a criminal case against Mary Boone, despite the fact that he claims that she told him he was getting the 1996 version but passed him the 2010 copy. There must be more to the case than has been made public, because otherwise this sounds like reasonable grounds for a fraud case.

Many are surprised that there is no crime called "forgery." Most forgers and their accomplices are tried for the crime of fraud and, in order to have committed a crime, a person or institution must have been victimized, defrauded (usually out of money). This distinction explains why famous American art forger Mark Landis (about whom the documentary film *Art and Craft* was made) was able to pass off more than forty forged paintings to museums and universities but never actually committed a crime: he never accepted money for them, giving them as gifts, so no one was defrauded.

Yet in this case, it seems clear that there was an attempt to fool Baldwin. He denies ever having been told that he was receiving a different work, though Boone's lawyer, Ted Poretz, stated, "By the time Alec Baldwin paid for the painting and it was delivered to him, he should not have misunderstood what he purchased." That is a particularly contorted sentence, one that sounds like it was carefully constructed to be truthful, while masking the grislier details of the story. He goes on to say, "[Baldwin's] wrong that the painting is a copy; it's an original and very fine work by Ross Bleckner." Poretz is half right: it is a very fine original work by Ross Bleckner and a copy. More damning, however, is the fact that the 2010 work was dated 1996, and the numbered stamp on the back of the canvas matched that of the 1996 version. That sounds like fraud to me.

So the real mystery is whatever we have not yet learned about the case that makes the DA say that a criminal case cannot be made. Baldwin has been offered a full refund, but instead he is demanding the 1996 version he had paid for and expected to receive. It remains to be seen whether the current owner ever actually considered selling the work, or whether this was all smoke and mirrors over *Sea and Mirror*.

Why Do Museums Fall for Forgeries?

Mark Landis created over forty mediocre forgeries and successfully passed them off to museums, yet he never seems to have committed a crime. The forgeries were bad enough that the museums recognized that they were fraudulent within hours of Landis leaving the premises. He never committed a crime, because no one was defrauded, since the museum so quickly realized they'd been gifted a forgery, and no one lost money or reputation. But these museums did accept the gifts the unusual Landis brought them and only checked to see what the gift (which, at first glance, looked alright) really looked like after the generous donor had gone.

When I teach the history of art crime, I'm often asked what percentage of museum collections are likely forgeries. I've read bold statistics that claim that some 10 or 20 percent of the displayed works in famous museums are forgeries. This is, of course, not true, or at least not verifiable. The short answer is that we don't know—and if we did know, then that percentage of forgeries on display would be 0, because, well, we would know that they were forgeries and they would be removed. The truth is that what goes on display at museums is, I'd guess about 98 percent of the time, just what the wall copy claims it to be. Perhaps some 10 to 20 percent of all of a museum's holdings are of uncertain authorship or were, at some point, misattributed, but these works are usually kept in storage. When I taught a seminar on art crime at Yale, we visited the Yale Art Gallery's storerooms, where my students could examine several identified forgeries, kept for didactic purposes. Only the near-certainties are displayed to the public. To understand why, we must make a distinction between fakes, forgeries, and misattributions.

In everyday parlance, we tend to use these terms interchangeably, all meaning a work of art that is not what the experts claim it to be. But in criminological terms, they are different, as I detail in my book *The Art of Forgery*. Both "fakes" and "forgeries" imply malice of forethought, and a proactive attempt at fraud by a criminal. This is extremely rare, which is why it makes headlines when it does happen (and when it is found out, an even rarer occurrence), as in the recent Modigliani affair. The discovery of forgeries and forgers is, to the art world, what the hunt for serial killers is to homicide detectives. The outlier that intrigues, breaks news, piques interest, but is so rare that, by virtue of its rarity alone, is newsworthy.

What happens far more often, so often that it is not particularly exciting beyond the confines of art specialists, is accidental misattribution. In short, this is a mistake made by experts who think that a work is by Artist X, when in fact it turns out to be by someone else (though the moment we learn that it is by someone else, its attribution changes and the problem is solved). This was particularly the case in the pre-Internet era, when many collections were purchased on behalf of nonexpert wealthy collectors by buyers abroad. In the seventeenth century, King Philip IV of Spain sent Diego Velázquez on a mission to Italy to buy up paintings for the royal collection. In the late nineteenth century and early twentieth, wealthy American collectors—the likes of Morgan, Frick, Ford, and Gardner—relied on agents to comb the galleries and monasteries and auction houses and private homes of Europe, looking for great art. The cost was little matter, as the collectors had far vaster wealth than the impecunious aristocrats of Europe, who were obliged to sell off their art to sustain their lifestyles. If an agent spotted a painting that looked like it might be a Rembrandt and telegraphed back to their wealthy patron saying that they've found a lovely Rembrandt, they would make a sale (and usually they were paid by commission). But if the agent honestly thought that it looked like school of Rembrandt, or in the style of Rembrandt, or maybe by Rembrandt but they couldn't be sure, and telegraphed back their honest uncertainty, they'd be unlikely to make the sale. Mr. Frick back in New York doesn't want to adorn his walls with a work "possibly by Rembrandt." He wants masterpieces and is happy to pay for them. Which is why you get collections pocked with question marks (and why *The Polish Rider* in the Frick collection is variously attributed to Rembrandt, circle of Rembrandt, style of Rembrandt, school of Rembrandt, and so on . . . a vocabulary of hierarchical uncertainty). One might think that experts should "know better," but attribution includes a healthy measure of subjective opinion and guesswork. Forensic tests can sometimes spot an anachronism that makes a work unlikely to be authentic, but they can very rarely prove authorship. And when you have the often-varying opinions of many experts, waters can get muddied.

There is also the phenomenon in the art world of not looking proverbial gift horses in the mouth, as we noted at the start of this essay. Museums regularly augment their permanent collections with donations and loans from patrons. Sometimes the permanent collections are very modest, indeed, and the highlights of museums may be loan objects. Patrons receive kudos and social points for supporting museums and can also receive benefits like tax deductions, while museums get new works to decorate their walls. It's a symbiotic system. When the odd oddity occurs, as in the case of Landis, who enjoyed feeling catered to for the few hours that he presented himself as a patron and donated an "artwork" to a collection, but who accepted no money or any other benefit in exchange, we see where there's a chink in the art world's armor. Museums rely on gifts and loans, and they are grateful enough for them that they don't always look as closely as perhaps they should to ensure that what is coming their way is what it claims to be.

And so it was with the twenty or so Modigliani forgeries displayed at the Palazzo Ducale Genoa exhibit, recently outed as forgeries. Whether the curator, currently under investigation, was a knowing party or just fooled remains a question, but curators are often fooled, due to enthusiasm, wishful thinking, or sometimes desperation to add content, especially promising, big-name works, to a collection or exhibit.

When I gave a talk at the Dulwich Picture Gallery while on tour to promote my *Art of Forgery* book, the museum had a promotion in place. The curators intentionally placed one forgery in the gallery's collection and challenged visitors to spot it. It was the gallery's most successful campaign to date. The irony is that the whiff of forgery, while dangerous to the reputations of the experts who were fooled, is catnip for the public. While twenty forgeries in a single show is a bit much, perhaps every exhibit should hide a single forgery within it for folks to enjoy trying to spot?

Reflections on Ghent's Blockbuster Van Eyck Exhibit

The 2020 *Van Eyck: An Optical Revolution* was the latest in a series of blockbuster exhibitions held in the Lowlands to feature their local artist heroes. In 2016 's-Hertogenbosch mounted a once-in-a-generation show bringing together almost all the works by Hieronymus Bosch. In 2018 Antwerp hosted a Rubens show, in 2019 there was a Brueghel show in Brussels, and now 2020 focuses on Jan van Eyck in Ghent, the home of his most important work, *Adoration of the Mystic Lamb* (1426–1432), aka *The Ghent Altarpiece*. The show brings together almost all of the artist's extant works, which will not happen again this century—securing such loans is hugely complicated, so this is your only chance to see them in one place.

It is easier to list the Van Eyck works that are not there, than those that are. For whatever reasons (expense, insurance, politics) the paintings from the National Gallery in London (*The Marriage Contract*, *Portrait of a Man in a Red Turban*) are missing, as is *The Madonna of Chancellor Rolin* from the Louvre. The other big guns are present and accounted for. Van Eyck lived in Bruges, but his masterpiece is *The Ghent Altarpiece*, an enormous triptych, comprised of twelve panels (some of them painted on both sides), weighing 1,500 kilos, so this is the most natural place for a retrospective on his work. The altarpiece is on many a list of superlatives: the first great work in oil painting, the first work of artistic realism, it was the most famous painting in Europe when it was completed, the most iconographically complicated, and a point of pilgrimage for artists and thinkers.

From 2012 to 2019, most of the altarpiece was painstakingly restored, layers of overpaint, past bad restorations and cloudy, dulling varnishes removed. The restoration led to some major changes to the appearance of the altarpiece. For instance, in a skyline in the background of one panel, a cluster of buildings were found that had been painted out, and details of other buildings come into focus, making them easier to identify with real, historical structures. The headline-grabbing detail was the face of the Mystic Lamb in the central panel. It used to have four ears, due to damage in a fire in 1822, and a restoration that led to the painting of a second face of the lamb over the original. The recent restoration removed the 1823 overpainting, including the extra set of ears, and revealed a lamb's face, as painted by Van Eyck, that is shockingly humanoid.

The exhibit (February 1–April 30), at MSK, the Fine Art Museum of Ghent, is a bestseller, to say the least. When I arrived, it was just two weeks into the show and they had already sold 170,000 tickets, were selling some 7,000 reservations a day, and only expected a maximum of 250,000 visitors. So I was very happy to return to Ghent, a city I love and have visited many times, and to see what all the fuss was about. I brought along a friend, the well-known Slovenian artist JAŠA (his artist name is indeed in all caps), as I was curious to learn the perspective of a contemporary conceptual artist on one of the great Old Masters.

"Look," says JAŠA, "he had trouble with the perspective in his paintings of legs, and he figured out a clever way to cover this up." Van Eyck having trouble with perspective? I'd never read that and it sounded almost sacrilegious to say, but he was right. The rear leg of Adam and of Eve, in their respective altarpiece panels, were tucked away behind the leg in front, as if not to have to deal with them. And the perspective was off. True, these panels would only be viewed from below, so that had to be taken into consideration, but they still looked hidden away, painted so as not to have to deal with them. Then we turned to Van Eyck's pair of small Saint Francis receiving the stigmata paintings (almost identical but one slightly largely than the other), and in both versions, the saint's left leg, farther from us viewers as he kneels facing right, looks dislocated. The perspective of legs gave him trouble. It took a painter to see what a painter struggled with.

Van Eyck's training and early practice as a miniaturist, illuminating Books of Hours with tiny paintings full of tinier details, is on full display. There are illuminations attributed to him, and to his relative, Barthelemy d'Eyck (his brother and sister were also in the family business). It is ideal to see these miniatures beside his midsized works and his colossal altarpiece panels. He was simply the first to transfer the detail work of miniatures, and the particular skill set needed to paint them, onto a larger scale. How the panels of *The Ghent Altarpiece* must have felt like a luxuriance of space to him, after his early career hemmed in by playing-card-sized spaces, or smaller.

"He clearly absolutely loved the painting process, but relished the details," JAŠA continues. "I can see that he blocked out aspects of each panel in the altarpiece fairly quickly, with blocks of paint that he did not bother to smooth out. This makes them recede and the intricate, polished detail work really jump out." When examining this closely, I could really see how select details were just sketched in with colors, a swath of paint with visible brushstrokes, whereas others were in magnifying-glass, brilliant finish.

And what detail. You can see individual hairs on Adam's arm, pores on his nose, hundreds of botanically identifiable plants, over one hundred figures each with a unique face (the tradition at the time was to use a generic face in religious paintings), the light shining off and through rubies and pearls. The panels of the altarpiece are disassembled for display here and provided the focal points, supplemented by other works by Van Eyck and his contemporaries.

I was in Ghent to speak at a conference on the many crimes in which *The Ghent Altarpiece* was the object (some thirteen different disasters, and it was stolen, all or in part, six or seven times, depending on your definition of theft, making it by far the world's most-frequently stolen artwork—the *Guinness Book of World Records* has it wrong, giving the title to Rembrandt's *Portrait of Jacob de Gheyn III*, stolen "only" four times). My 2010 book, *Stealing the Mystic Lamb*, was a sort of biography of the painting, which is easy to argue was the most important painting ever made, and its dramatic adventures as a desired object. So I was also wandering the gallery with colleagues from the security and policing fields, including Ibrahim Bulut, who worked as a security specialist on this exhibit. He pointed out the revolutionary use of lighting employed here, a benchmark for future exhibits, including the highest-grade lights for jewelry displays mounted inside the protective glass cases. Other cases were spot-lit from above but the tops were made of opaque glass, which diffused the spotlight, mimicking daylight inside the case and eliminating any glare. The exhibit is ingeniously curated, with the wall copy text shifted higher up on the wall, so crowds can read it easily without jostling those trying to look at the art. Historical objects were found to display next to Van Eyck's paintings of similar such objects, with an emphasis on how the light falls on the objects themselves (a blown-glass decanter for water, a brass washbasin) and how Van Eyck got it just right.

The focus of the exhibit is "An Optical Revolution" and that is really what struck most. Dr. Maximilien Martens, a Van Eyck specialist at University of Ghent, pointed out how Van Eyck's main stylistic goal was to reproduce the play of light—its reflections, refractions, optics—in paint. He showed a slow-motion video of water dropping into a water-filled basin, how each drop smashes into the water in the basin, creates a depression, and then catapults droplets into the air, which in turn crash back into the basin. We can only see this with a video in slo-mo, but Van Eyck managed to paint this effect exactly as it looks in the freeze-frame of the video. "He clearly had photographic memory," JAŠA says, "and an eye for remembering details that pass so quickly that most of us are not aware of them." In the "Knights of Christ" panel of the altarpiece, we see three types of reflections in one suit of armor. A knight is carrying a red lance, and we see the reflection of the lance "broken" into halves as it bends over his angled breastplate; then we see sunlight reflected against his convex shield, and again reflected off his convex, round shoulder guard. In the altarpiece panel depicting Mary in the Annunciation, she is shown kneeling before an open book, the Old Testament, of which just three words are visible. They translate as "As God sees." And this is really what both the exhibit and Van Eyck's passion are all about. The ability to produce paintings that provide a God's-eye-view of the world, from macroscopic (a field of hundreds of figures paying homage to the Mystic Lamb) to microscopic (reflection of light in a horse's eye, pores on someone's nose). The ability to get so close to the paintings, to zoom in on details, was something I'd never before experienced. I had actually learned more from examining a zoomable five-billion-pixel digital image of *The Ghent Altarpiece* than I ever had looking at it in person.

One of the lasting impressions that surprised me was how I felt badly for Van Eyck's famous Italian contemporaries, whose paintings were displayed alongside his: Fra Angelico, Domenico Veneziano, Masaccio. They looked so basic, simple, primitive in comparison, terms I never thought I would apply to the Cinquecento greats. "Their finished paintings look like a preparatory step in Van Eyck's process," JAŠA commented. It's true, their works looked like the more basic, blocked-out forms that Van Eyck would hone with further, scalpel-thin layers of detail. The main difference was in the medium—most of the Cinquecento Italian works were in tempera, rather than oil, and the media stand alongside each other in stark contrast. Oil simply allows for so much more detail that tempera looks like a blunt instrument.

As we approached the last room of the exhibit, I grew confused. Where was the rest of the altarpiece? The exhibit was set up for the final room to be a great climax, the newly cleaned *Adoration of the Mystic Lamb* central panel on full display, as well as the yet-to-be-cleaned monumental figures of Mary, Christ Enthroned (interpreted by some scholars as God the Father), and John the Baptist. But the exhibit just ended, rather abruptly. To see the main panels of the altarpiece, we had to go across town to Saint Bavo's Cathedral, where they had been returned after the five-year restoration.

This was anticlimactic, but understandable. The cathedral had been without its famous altarpiece for many years, and I am told that it was a sort of political issue between the cathedral, the city, and the museum that meant that the central panels would return to the cathedral, even while the wing panels were part of this three-month exhibit at the museum.

The next morning, JAŠA and I headed over to Saint Bavo's Cathedral. We expected a line, since the MSK exhibit was so overbooked, but there was none, just the average number of tourists I was used to seeing in past visits. It might be argued that it is good to keep the altarpiece in situ, and I'm always in favor of this, though it is not quite where it was meant to be. It was designed and painted for the Joost Vijd Chapel in the cathedral, but it was moved to a space adjacent to the entrance. Stepping inside, as I've done countless times over my many visits to the see the artwork, was different now than before. It was in contrast to the immaculate, brilliant architecture, lighting, and installation of the MSK exhibit that the space that houses the central panels looked so gloomy, downtrodden, inappropriate.

Part of the delight in seeing such details at the MSK exhibit came from the contrast to the way the altarpiece is displayed at Saint Bavo's Cathedral, in a cumbersome protective case with at least a meter and a half (five feet) between the glass and the altarpiece. That's a lot of real estate separating our eyes from the painting itself. With today's security technologies, there is no need for such a case—the work could be just as well protected with a case that is like those used in this exhibit, with robust security glass that looks delicate and allows us to get inches from the painting. JAŠA pointed out a simple detail: on the floor beside the altarpiece was a cheap, gray plastic trashcan with a plastic liner bag squished into it. Posters on the wall, printed in basic paper, were splotchy and browned.

The lighting was very poor—the three monumental figures enthroned in Heaven were in shadow, barely visible. I had never noticed the shabbiness of the display until it was contrasted to the beauty of the MSK exhibit. In October 2020, Saint Bavo's is opening a new visitors' center for the altarpiece, and I can only hope that this will coincide with an improved display of the altarpiece itself.

2 LAW, POLICING, AND POLICY

Is Marina Abramović Trying to Erase Ulay from the History of Art?

A tall, bearded old man with the weathered, craggy face of a handsome, kindly sea captain stands in a pale pink negligée in a gallery in Amsterdam's Stedelijk Museum. As part of his January 15, 2015, performance, portentously entitled *A Skeleton in the Closet*, he inscribes clusters of numbers onto a pale pink square upon the wall: 252, 253, 288, 289. The sell-out 120 spectators who made it in ahead of the 500 or so hopefuls outside the gallery try to discern what it all could mean. Is Ulay referencing astrology? Crypto-numerology?

The tall old man was born as Frank Uwe Laysiepen but has worked for more than fifty years as Ulay. He is one of the most important artists of the second half of the twentieth century, so influential that he is one of only three or four conceptual artists included in most standard introduction to art history textbooks. The only twentieth-century conceptual artist who is perhaps better known is Marina Abramović, Ulay's partner in life and art from 1976 until 1988, when they dramatically and poetically split up after a performance in which each set out from opposite ends of the Great Wall of China and met in the middle for a farewell. Ulay is a legend in the contemporary art world but never sought more mainstream acclaim. Abramović, on the other hand, shot from the status of important artist to household name thanks to a 2010 retrospective at MoMA in New York and a major documentary film (*The Artist Is Present*, 2012), after which she began hanging out with people like Jay-Z and Lady Gaga, and making Adidas commercials. It is Marina who is the subject of those numbers that feature in Ulay's recent pale pink performance.

What was once the storybook romance of the art world has long since soured. Now Ulay alleges that Marina is in breach of a contract they signed in 1999, detailing how to handle their joint oeuvre. He has brought a lawsuit against her, which was tried in Amsterdam in 2015. The behind-the-scenes issues between Marina and Ulay have never been made public before, nor has the court case, which, Ulay explained in a series of interviews exclusive to the *Guardian*, is about the enforcement of their existing contract. But their troubles go beyond matters of finance and transparency—for it seems that Marina is trying to exert control over Ulay's artistic legacy and even write his name out of the history books.

The most famous works in the oeuvres of Marina and Ulay are those they did together, and there are scores of them. These include *Incision* (1978), in which a naked Ulay repeatedly ran toward a clothed Marina but was blocked and pushed back by an elastic rope; *AAA-AAA* (1978) in which Ulay and Marina, face to face, screamed "AAA" at one another at the top of their lungs; *Relation in Space* (1976) in which they ran into each other, naked, across a gallery space for an hour; *Imponderabilia* (1977) in which they stood naked opposite each other in the narrow doorway of a gallery, so that visitors had to turn sideways to squeeze past them and choose which one to face in doing so; and the wonderfully inflammatory *Irritation: There Is a Criminal Touch to Art* (1976), in which they stole a painting from a Berlin museum and documented the process.

Their relationship is such a key part of the history of performance and body art that their knot can never be unwoven, symbolized (though surely inadvertently) through their 1977 *Relation in Time*, in which they performed bound together by their braided hair—but facing away from one another. Evidence of the endurance of the very idea of their relationship (even among those unfamiliar with their art) may be seen in a viral video of a moment during Marina's performance at MoMA in 2010, in which visitors were invited to sit quietly opposite her. As a surprise, Ulay stood in line and eventually took his place before her. Both grew teary over the few minutes during which they sat, staring at one another. The editor of the video (which was made and distributed without the permission of either artist) added some explicatory text and dramatic music, making the video seem like the reunification of long-lost lovers. The video has twenty-two million viewers and counting. But today matters are not quite as romantic as the video would lead one to believe.

Now aged seventy-one as I write this, Ulay lives in Amsterdam and Ljubljana (he has since passed away, but I wrote this piece in 2015). Warm and soft-spoken, with a haggard, bearded handsomeness, Ulay seems to have more stories in his life than could fit in one biography. He was born in Germany but is synonymous with Amsterdam's art scene, where he lived for decades and still keeps an apartment. His art career began with his role as an official photographer for Polaroid, using their colossal 20 x 24 camera to take pictures as he traversed Europe. The majority of his oeuvre remains photographic, but he shot to fame through his performances, which have often brought gender roles into question, with Ulay frequently cross-dressing (indeed, he did a piece for *Zoo* magazine in which he revisited this youthful theme, now with his elderly body as his canvas). He was the subject of a 2013 documentary film, *Project Cancer*, which followed him for a year after he was diagnosed with cancer—which he managed to beat. In 2014, he came out with a book, *Whispers: Ulay on Ulay*, which contains numerous interviews with him and essays about his work, as well as images of his complete works. At least, it was supposed to contain images of his complete works.

From 1988 to 1999, Marina and Ulay did not speak. Having fallen out and separated, the onetime partners needed to find a way to manage their combined oeuvre, which was considerable, in extent, importance, and financial worth. During that time, the large works were in Marina's possession (like the oversized 20 x 24 Polaroids), while Ulay had the smaller archival objects (like photographic negatives). Ulay managed their joint archive, but it required a lot of administration and he was less than proactive on the business side of things. At the encouragement of Marina's New York gallerist, Sean Kelly, a contract was drawn up and filed in Amsterdam, where Ulay long resided, prepared by a Dutch lawyer and an American law firm, that laid out how their oeuvre should be dealt with. Ulay sold his physical archive of their joint projects to Marina for a flat fee, which included exploitation rights. That physical archive, now entirely in Marina's possession, could be used to produce saleable work at Marina's discretion (for instance, photographs made from negatives or copies of video art). But Marina would have to inform Ulay of any of their joint material that was either sold or to be exhibited. Any net income generated would go 50 percent to the gallery (standard in the art world), with 20 percent going to Ulay and 30 percent to Marina. All fairly straightforward, and both parties seemed satisfied, although when the agreement was made, Ulay did not want to meet with Marina in person, so Sean Kelly acted as intermediary.

Since 1999, this contract has been only loosely adhered to, as Ulay describes during our conversations in Ljubljana: "There is a lot of money going through her accounts, and of course they have a very good accountant." But Ulay has received surprisingly little, for Marina had occasionally sent Ulay his cut of the earnings on their joint works calculated in a very different way from the contract stipulations. Instead of 20 percent of the total income going to Ulay, he explains, Marina was giving him 20 percent of her 30 percent, or around 6 percent of the total. "A few weeks ago, I got from her again that she has sold etc., etc., and I'm entitled to get 20 percent of her 30 percent. We don't agree." This is just one of the transgressions of the contract, as Ulay tells it. In the past, the finances might not have been a big issue. But since her 2010 MoMA exhibition, she has become far more proactive in producing work, but Ulay has received little income from it or information about it, both of which the contract stipulates he is due. He says that he only received three sales statements in all that time (once in 2008 and twice in 2012) and received payment only four times over the course of sixteen years, for a total income of around thirty-three thousand euros (when each of their works sell regularly for five to six figures). Only one of those four payments was correctly calculated, he explains, with Ulay receiving 20 percent of the net total. The others were calculated at 20 percent of her 30 percent cut. "I must admit to something that has led to this whole unsolved problem," Ulay says, "and that is my own initial indifference. Because I don't want to always struggle with her." There was certainly more income generated than Ulay was made aware of. For instance, he says that he only learned of a major Adidas commercial in which their joint work was reenacted when it was being filmed. Only because Ulay sent her a pointed letter did her lawyers insist that she add his name to the commercial in postproduction. Ulay describes the main points that he hopes the lawsuit will require of her, none of which are new: "My whole court case is to stick to our agreement," enforcing the preexisting contract. "The points I'm asking of her are: every six months, a statement about sales and my royalties from the sales. I'm asking for absolute proper mentioning of my name. I'm asking her to write a letter to all her galleries about name mentioning," giving proper credit for coauthored works.

But the money, while a breach of contract, is the least of it. What really concerns Ulay is his perception that Marina is trying to rewrite history, and airbrush him out of it. Their contract stipulates how their joint works must be credited: the artists listed as "Ulay/Abramović" for works made in their earlier period, 1976–1980, when Ulay was the more prominent name, and as "Abramović/Ulay" for works made from 1981 to 1988. This, Ulay claims, she has rarely done, taking sole authorship credit for some of their re-performances. "She's not just a former business partner. The whole oeuvre has made history. It's now in schoolbooks. But she has deliberately misinterpreted things, or left my name out. But I had never reacted, because I wanted to have peace of mind." Until now.

Ulay says that he might never have reacted, had Marina not tried to interfere with his book. He was shaken from his torpor in 2013. Marina had given an interview, to be included in Ulay's book, *Whispers*, which was published in December 2014 by a small Dutch art publisher, Valiz. But when she received the PDF proofs of the book, in April 2013, something happened. "When she saw the PDF," Ulay explains, "she engaged a lawyer and approached the publisher, not me." Marina had her lawyer send an official letter to the publisher, claiming that she had not given permission to use either the interview or the images (though technically Ulay did not require her permission to use the images, only to inform her of their use). This was particularly spiteful, because the book was originally conceived as a possible elegy to Ulay. One of its authors, Maria Rus Bojan, explains, "Ulay commissioned me to make this book before he started the chemotherapy for his lymphoma. We were all very much afraid that he would not survive the treatment." Rus Bojan flew to New York to personally ask Abramović to be interviewed for the book. "She was extremely kind," Rus Bojan recalls, "that was in 2012, during Ulay's treatment." It is that much stranger, then, that Abramović would make such a sudden about-face and threaten the publisher with litigation.

The publisher panicked and, fearing a lawsuit, quickly established a foundation that would officially publish *Whispers*—a foundation with no capital to lose, as a tactical measure, and which would be distinct from the rest of her publishing house. The interview had been undertaken expressly for the book, and this was very late in the day to make objections, with the book scheduled for printing. In consultation with Ulay's lawyers, it was determined that Marina did not have the right to block the publication of images from their joint oeuvre. But to avoid a potentially messy and expensive lawsuit, which the publisher was particularly keen to steer clear of, it was decided that a fixed number of the images of their joint works had been published and republished so many times that citation rights applied, and their inclusion was beyond objection. "It was such a mean thing to do," Ulay laments, "because most of the images had been published elsewhere before." Indeed, as Amelia Jones, a professor at the University of Southern California, notes, "The irony of course is that all such images are freely available over the Internet. So the person refusing permission and calling lawyers is exposed as being self-serving and controlling." Those works which had rarely, or never, been published (the inclusion of which was one of the selling points of the book) were potentially problematic. Ulay decided to exclude those images but include the information about them (title, location, date), publishing instead a pale pink square on each page, the exact dimensions of the withdrawn image. No explanation was offered in the book itself of this striking oddity, aside from a brief note hidden in the acknowledgments at the back: "Marina Abramović has objected to the use of the images of the joint works Ulay/Abramović or Abramović/Ulay for this publication. Although we believe that a book about Ulay would be incomplete without a selection of their joint works, and the use of such images is permitted under the citation right, we have nonetheless felt obliged to cover a number of the images with pink or black fields." Ulay expresses surprise that he has never once been asked about these pinked-out images by a member of the media. But it did have an effect on Marina, as Ulay notes: "I think it must have pissed her off."

There were several concerns that had been eating away at Ulay, and which now came to the fore. First was what Ulay describes as an ongoing lack of transparency in the exhibition and sale of their joint works. Marina has reenacted some of their joint performances without his permission. Ulay even points out that the title of Marina's famous MoMA performance, *The Artist Is Present*, was actually copped from his very first performance, in Amsterdam. "In her show, *The Artist Is Present*, which she put on at MoMA, the title should have been *The Artist Is Not Present*," Ulay jokes, though without mirth. "You know what the title was of my first show ever, in 1974? *The Artist Is Present*." There was also the issue of being underpaid. This was particularly odd because, in her biography, Marina explains the finances correctly—that Ulay should receive 20 percent net (as is written in their contract, which the *Guardian* examined as part of this essay, which first ran there). Now she contests this. Marina also seemed to object to Ulay's establishment of a foundation that would be the financial beneficiary of his works, and which would in turn pay royalties to his three children. This is standard among established artists, to set up a foundation to supervise their legacy and handle their estate once they are gone, and Marina has her own version of this, the Marina Abramović Institute. "I want the whole estate to go into the Ulay Foundation," Ulay says, "and the foundation will be cared for by a number of people. She was against this too. She has no heirs. She'd want her institute to take over my estate." Along with her frequent neglect to give him proper credit on their joint works, this foundation matter may be another symptom of what is the main issue for Ulay, which is the sense that Marina is trying to write him out of their joint history. Amelia Jones adds, "It's impressive, actually, the degree to which she has been able to produce narratives of the history of performance that serve to build up her position in that history. For example, the media repeatedly calls her the 'mother' or 'grandmother' of performance art, as if Carolee Schneemann, Shigeko Kubota, Yoko Ono, Valie Export, and many other women weren't already doing performance art in the 1960s and early 1970s before Abramović emerged!" Could the "grandmother of performance art" really wish to diminish, if not erase, the role of the "grandfather"?

If the financial issue, and those related to proper accreditation, has been an ongoing one since the contract was signed, sixteen years ago, then why this sudden, unfriendly, and confrontational attitude regarding permission to include her interview and images in his book? A relationship that passionate, between two such deeply sensitive artists, would always have its ups and downs, and the intensity of their love affair, the interreliance of creativity that it produced, was destined to lead to hard feelings when it ended. But their post-breakup relations remained cordial and understanding, even through a period without communication. If there were instances when Ulay felt that the business side of their collaborative production was masked to him, or if he didn't receive as much as he probably should, it never reached a boiling point.

But then, in April 2013, two things happened that seemed to break whatever fragile peace Marina had in her approach toward Ulay. "For the film [*Project Cancer*] she was collaborative, it was still okay, she didn't feel threatened," Ulay explains. "But with the book [*Whispers: Ulay on Ulay*], with my works before and after . . . she wanted to be the only star, like I was nothing before her and nothing after." On the one hand, Ulay was about to come out with his book, the first to authoritatively write his side of the story of his art (neither traditional biography nor autobiography, the book is a collage of interviews with Ulay and essays, accompanied by images of his complete works). Marina had long been the more vocal and the more written about, at least in the public eye (Ulay has always been the subject of art critics and historians, but not the household name Marina became after her 2010 retrospective and documentary film). Ulay was seizing the reins of his own history, and their mutual one. "It seems like revenge," suggests Maria Rus Bojan. "Marina has seen herself always as the driving force behind their collaborative work. By refusing Ulay's moral rights on publishing his own work in his own monograph—that was a declaration of war." As Ulay says, "I was hurt, very much hurt. It is unthinkable, so unjust, so not right. When I was working with her, she was great. But then, you know, the direction she went to, to become an artist/star, is something I do not envy. It's far away from my intentions, wishes, desires. But it went to her head."

That was the professional side. But there is the key event that took place after the book was in progress: Ulay got married in 2013. That was after Marina had voluntarily been interviewed for the book, but before the book was due to come out—soon after she rescinded permission to use the interview. Read into the psychology of the matter what you will, but the timing suggests that this event proved difficult for Marina to swallow. Her exertion of authority over what Ulay would be permitted to publish about his own life, coupled with the longstanding questions regarding the transparency and fairness of her handling of their mutual oeuvre, finally led Ulay to legal action. It does not take a psychologist to see that the things Marina is objecting to, and that caused her to bristle, have to do with Ulay definitively taking his life and story into his own hands, distinct from his onetime partner. Writing his own history, establishing his own foundation, finally marrying. These are markers of independence that go beyond the simple distance of living and working apart: they are forever, and Marina has no control over them, and so flails to exert some influence over a man she may have never ceased to love.

Of course, Marina could never completely erase Ulay from the history of art—he has been written about so often, over so many decades, that his presence will be everlasting. As curator Tevz Logar says, "Marina cannot overpower Ulay and take credit, because every single person in the art world knows that the *Relation Works* [their most famous collaborative series] worked because of the balance between them, and of their equal and joint efforts. That is how it entered the history of art and performance." All she can do, as she has done, is try to throw a wrench into the gears of his personal projects, his attempts to write his own story and tend to his own legacy, independent of her. Logar continues, "I actually think that Marina's agenda here is more banal and pragmatic. Unlike Marina, Ulay never cared about maintaining his position in the contemporary art world and was never really a presence on the market. So when Ulay only recently started to be represented by MOT International, a progressive gallery in London and Brussels, that meant that he started to enter Marina's symbolic space, space that until now she ruled over." This was exemplified by Ulay's featured role at the world's most important contemporary art fair, Art Basel. As Logar concludes, all of a sudden the "grandmother of performance," after more than twenty years alone at the top of the market, is confronted by the "allegedly lost grandfather."

As they wait for the outcome of the legal wrangle, Ulay's career and prominence continue in ascendance. He says that Marina has already agreed to most of his requirements, but a few stumbling blocks remain. What has been shorn beyond repair, it seems, is the taut and fraught cord that braids together these two remarkable, ingenious, important artists who will forever be associated with one another. At least in the history books, and despite some concerted efforts.

The tall old man in the pink negligee writes numbers upon the pale pink square on the wall of the Stedelijk Museum. What are those numbers? Neither crypto-numerological nor astrological, they are something altogether more straightforward, but at the same time more emotionally complicated. They are the image and page numbers of the pinked-out, censored works in Ulay's book, the collaborative projects that half of the most influential tandem of conceptual artists in history refused to permit to be seen.

Remembering Ulay

Last night (March 2, 2020), Uwe Laysiepen, the influential photographer and conceptual and performance artist, passed away. While the art world will mourn the loss of one of the greats of the postmodern era, I will miss him as a wonderful, kind man who happened to be an ingenious artist.

Ulay, like me, married a beautiful Slovenian woman and settled down on the sunny side of the Alps, in Ljubljana. We met through mutual friends, Slovenia's most famous rock star, in fact, who threw a dinner party for us at his home. His wife prepared salt-baked fish and, as she cracked open the salt crust, I couldn't help but feel the gush of a groupie as I looked across the table, through the windowpane of steam, at a man whom I had studied in Art History 101.

Ulay was one of just a handful of living artists who are enshrined in most introduction to art history textbooks. You can find him in the last chapter, after you've combed over Lysippus and Giotto, Donatello and Michelangelo, Ingres and Picasso. There he is, usually in conjunction with his onetime long-term romantic and artistic partner, Marina Abramović. Their work as a duo was seminal to the course of performance art in the late 1970s and '80s, but they were also great artists in their separate careers. Ulay began as one of the few official photographers for Polaroid in the sixties. While we think of his performance art (he always preferred the German word, *Aktion*, or an action, rather than performance)—most iconically his 1976 art theft as artwork, *Irritation: There Is a Criminal Touch to Art*, when he successfully stole Hitler's favorite painting from a Berlin museum and brought it to hang on the wall of an impoverished Turkish immigrant family, before calling the authorities to come and retrieve it—he began as a photographer. His independent career also touched upon shifting genders, decades before this was à la mode. He invented a hybrid-gendered alter ego, Renais Sense, for which he made up one hemisphere of his face like a woman and the other like a man. He was a pioneer in body art, considering the body to be the artistic medium par excellence. Indeed, just last night, as it turns out he was dying, I was writing about him for a forthcoming book, featuring him in a chapter on shock as an artistic tactic. With Abramović, he explored the human body and its functions as artistic acts. In *Imponderabilia*, one of the most famous performance artworks of all time, he and Abramović stood, naked, in a narrow doorway within a gallery, forcing visitors to shimmy past them, sidling sideways, confronting either his nakedness or hers, in order to access the gallery space. Early works as a duo included a performance in which they took turns slapping each other, interested in the sound this made.

In another work, they repeatedly ran, naked, smashing into columns in a parking garage with their shoulders. The columns were unattached and had been rigged on sleds, so they would slide ever so slightly backward with each strike. But they were heavy and caused bruising, nonetheless. Later works examined the physical capabilities of the human body other than pain. *Nightsea Crossing* (1981–1987) was a series of twenty-two performances over a total of ninety days in which the two artists would sit opposite each other, completely still, for many hours at a time. Both practiced ayurvedic meditation and trained extensively for these performances, which required incredible concentration and mental strength. In extensive interviews I undertook with Ulay, he explained how they trained themselves to "scratch itches with our minds." The errant fly, not to mention audience members who made a game of trying to distract them (the way tourists might try to make a Buckingham Palace guard move from their rock-still stance), were among the obstacles.

Ulay and Abramović will always be intertwined, even though they eventually had a falling out. After the lawsuit, the two met by chance, or fate, at an ayurvedic retreat in rural India. Ulay was there with his talented wife, designer Lena Pislak, who has been his constant companion, support, and driving force for years now. But what could have been very awkward was not. The two artists decided to put the issue aside and became friendly again, against all odds. Years later, they even discussed writing a joint memoir together.

After his split with Abramović, he continued to work and cultivate relationships with a younger generation of artists, curators, gallerists, and people like me, an art historian. Artist JAŠA performed with Ulay in New York in 2016. *Cutting through the Clouds of Myth* was Ulay's first performance after a more than twenty-five-year hiatus, and it was much anticipated, but no more so than by his collaborator, an artist almost half his age, who notes, "His focus, his presence was a unique experience."

There was a fatherly guru vibe about him. When he would email or text me, he would call me "Dear." He and I conducted some twenty hours of interviews with the idea of doing a book together, an insider's-eye-view of conceptual art in the second half of the twentieth century, but he passed away before we could move further. He took up activist causes, calling himself an "artivist" for clean water. He spoke poetically, eloquently, with the sort of phrases that you want to jot down, or carve in stone, falling like water from his lips, even in casual conversation. He once said, "One can learn many things in life, but not art. The madness you need—the must which is shaking you all the time. You are an artist even when you are asleep. Because of the must." He was an artist to the bone.

His legacy will be kept illuminated by the Ulay Foundation, which opened last year in Ljubljana. It includes a gallery space and will host residencies for artist couples. "My entire artistic practice," Ulay said, "is rooted in the belief that art has the capacity to contribute to life." The goal of his foundation is to continue his legacy and support others who use art to contribute to life.

Ulay was, above all, a man of enormous warmth and kindness. I spent countless hours at his kitchen table in his sunny Ljubljana apartment, sharing his Marlboros and drinking a special healthful brew, which he liked to call his magic potion, that Lena prepared for him. He had beaten cancer twice already (once documented in the film *Project Cancer*). Each time, he had gone on an ayurvedic retreat and that, combined with the help of the respected oncology clinic in Ljubljana, had sent his cancer into remission. Against all odds, with the loving support of those closest to him, he remained remarkably active, even in sickness. He said, "Death is the ultimate answer. But life is absolute."

At one time he had considered his illness and the documentation of it as a type of performance.

It would be his ultimate *Aktion*.

Is That Eames an Original? Inside Industrial Design Wars

The confusion began when I inherited my father's original Eames lounge chair, the sort that has cushioned psychiatrists like him for decades. He'd bought it with his first big paycheck, as a young psychiatrist back in the 1960s, when Charles and Ray Eames, arguably the most famous of American industrial designers, were at their peak—and still living. Renovating a house myself, and wishing to furnish it with a similar midcentury modern aesthetic, I wanted to buy other items by Eames and other designers I admire, the aesthetic all-stars whose creations are ubiquitous, although you might not know them by name, if you are neither an architect nor a design geek, the likes of Isamu Noguchi, Vernon Panton, Hans Coray, and Jean Prouvé. But a quick Internet search left me stumped. Take the iconic Eames DSW Eiffel chair, which I thought would be nice for our dining room table. I found scores of chairs on various online stores, all labeled identically and looking (at first glance, at least) identical, but with price ranges all over the map, from four hundred to forty euros. Some websites indicated that they sold replicas, others did not. Having recently published a book on art forgery, my interest was immediately piqued.

My first port of call for Eames DSW Eiffel chairs was the nearest official Vitra retailer, a store called Kubus, in Ljubljana, near my home. Ula Vehovar, of Kubus, told me, "People who wouldn't even think of buying a fake handbag, watch, or sunglasses lower their standards dramatically when it comes to furniture. Authorities, who very efficiently intercept shipments of counterfeit cigarettes or sports goods, see no problem in containers of replicas arriving from the Far East." The Swiss Vitra firm has long held the license to distribute "original" Eames chairs in Europe, paying the Eames estate and the original producer of the chair, American firm Herman Miller, for the privilege, and enjoying a relationship with the designers dating back to the 1960s. These chairs, one imagines, are exactly as the designers intended, aesthetically and materially. But they also cost over four hundred euros each, which was out of our budget, since we were after six to eight of them for our dining room. I began to explore the replica options (though with a sense of nibbling at forbidden fruit) and found a vast number of them, with a similarly broad scale of quality and similarity to the original. This confused me, since I live in Europe, where the European Union has ostensibly strict laws protecting 3D design, like furniture, from unlicensed replication. The proliferation of replicas openly advertised online in mainland Europe, which has laws against them, suggests that the rules are confusing, loopholed, and inconsistently enforced. As lawyer Metod Žagar said, "Enforcing the rights holder of the design largely resembles tilting at windmills."

Most of the sites advertising replicas were in the United Kingdom. There are some that, even from an online photograph, are clearly different from the original: the legs are stouter; the bolts are a different color; the impression of the legs, like two dimples, is visible in the base of the seat. Others appear identical, even when looking at details (for instance, the originals have a groove in the L-shaped metal bracket that bolts the leg to the base, which is meant to provide added strength—one replica I examined had this, while most did not). My research also turned up some interesting, recent wrinkles to the story. The *Guardian* published an article about a company called Voga, which sells quality but extremely low-priced replicas. In May 2016, the company closed down in England and moved to Ireland. You can still order from their site, voga.com, but they require buyers to arrange their own shipping from a warehouse in Ireland—a fiddly, consumer-unfriendly policy that they appear to hide on their site and which they do not explain on it (they also did not reply to my attempts to reach them for this essay). This was explained by the *Guardian* as a way to circumvent strict EU design protection laws that the United Kingdom has just enforced, but from which Ireland remains exempt.

On July 28, 2016, a new law was passed in the United Kingdom, protecting the copyright of industrial designs, including Eames furniture, against copies of designs, as well as granting retrospective copyright protection to designs made prior to 1957, which were never copyrighted in the first place. The law brings the United Kingdom up to speed with the stricter EU laws and jurisprudence of the Court of Justice of the European Union. The previous UK law had stated that, twenty-five years after being created, designs could be reproduced. The new law, matching that of the European Union, states that copyright is in place for the life of the designer, plus seventy years. This not only will curb the sale of replicas but even applies to two-dimensional photographs of the original designs, which must not appear on websites.

If, that is, it is enforced.

This issue is hardly unique to the United Kingdom, but there have been some high-profile kerfuffles related to it of late. It came out that former prime minister David Cameron's wife, Samantha, bought a replica of Achille Castiglioni's Arco lamp for 250 GBP (originals cost 1,500), prompting the editor of *Elle Decoration* magazine to state that she was "cheap, hypocritical and fake" for her support of the "faux-furniture" industry.

But is this so wrong, if a replica is clearly labeled as such? In the world of fine art, there is no objection, legal or moral, to one artist producing work that copies another, so long as there is no attempt at fraud: copies, labeled as such and not mechanically but handmade, are considered acts of homage rather than theft. In the world of luxury goods, like Louis Vuitton handbags, the shape of the bag is not what is copyrighted, but the logos are—a Louis Vuitton–shaped handbag without any of the brand identifiers would be legal to produce. But industrial design, particularly iconic pieces like the Eames lounge chair, are iconic based on their overall shape and material—the logo has nothing to do with it.

In the United States, the laws appear simpler, but there is much room for interpretation, which can lead to confusion. While trademarks, logos, and patents are protected, Oxford law professor Graeme B. Dinwoodie wrote in *IPRinfo* magazine that "the United States doesn't have utility model laws, and it does not grant protection against slavish imitation: in the United States, that's called free competition." This means that firms can indeed approximate the designs of others, though without reproducing trademarked logos and, of course, without trying to pass them off as something they are not. Design patents can be registered but, Dinwoodie continues, they have "proven to be very unreliable." That is why the lawsuit between Samsung and Apple is particularly interesting. In January 2015, a US Court of Appeals reopened a longstanding patent lawsuit accused Samsung of copying the design of the Apple iPhone, the issues including the shape of the phone and its screen.

It remains to be seen if US laws will shift. Bringing the UK law in line with the rest of Europe was partly to do with Brexit, partly to do with the heavy lobbying of Vitra, which claimed to be losing a quarter billion euros per year to UK-based replicas of the designs for which they hold exclusive license. The scale of the market for these midcentury modern objects is enormous, though that number likely reflects estimated sales if all the people who bought low-priced replicas were to instead buy high-priced originals (which is financially improbable). One danger with such a law is that a black market in replicas will rise, for otherwise these products will only be available to the wealthy. This is rather ironic, because the stated goal of Charles and Ray Eames was to make great design available to the masses, indicating a desire for affordable products that laws seeking to protect designers have forced into a realm affordable only to the elite.

This new UK law has yet to be enforced in court. As lawyer Edgar Tijhuis notes, "According to transitional provisions, these sellers were still allowed to sell their existing stock of copies (or destroy them) until January 28, 2017. After this date, selling these same copies may actually constitute a serious infringement of copyright." Simon Ayrton, a partner at Powell Gilbert LLP in the United Kingdom, expects lawsuits in the near future to show that the law will be enforced: "Action may be taken against those that infringe copyright after the end of the transitional period." The period has passed, and yet replicas are still sold on a wide array of websites. It remains to be seen which firm will be targeted first, as an example to the rest. In Slovenia, only Kubus is allowed to sell Eames chairs, but that has not prevented replicas being advertised by other firms.

As an experiment for this essay, I bought a promising-looking replica that the seller assured me was identical to the original, for eighty-nine euros—a price I could handle. When it arrived, I was eager to test it. It looked just like the original I had seen in the licensed shop, retailing for over four hundred euros. It felt the same, too, when I sat in it. Extremely comfortable, supporting the lower back when sitting upright, giving just the right amount when leaning back. The legs were somewhat less elegant and elongated than the originals, and the bolts affixing them to the base were white, rather than black, the L-shaped brackets flat, not grooved. Regular use over time is the only way to determine whether this replica is "built to last." But the new laws mean that replicas will become rarer, more expensive, and more dangerous for producers, and it is possible that originals will rise in price, too, now without discounted competition.

Danish furniture company Fritz Hansen went public in condemnation of McDonald's for using replica Arne Jacobsen furniture, alongside originals, in its rebranded restaurant interiors. Hansen ceased supplying McDonald's, despite the huge income from doing so, stating that it "could not cooperate with a group that accepted piracy and set aside intellectual property rights." Though their purchases were not illegal, McDonald's wished to avoid bad publicity and will stick to originals. At a recent visit to a newly opened McDonald's, I noted that the chairs throughout were Eames DSW Eiffels. While my daughters enjoyed a Happy Meal, I surreptitiously flipped over a chair. Grooved brackets, black bolts. An original.

Museum of the Bible Is Busted

In 2015, I penned an article for the *Washington Post* that was the first to look inside the Green collection at the Museum of the Bible and profile the controversial museum's uncontroversial director, respected scholar David Trobisch. What had brought the museum to my attention was not only the headline-grabbing facts that it was to cost half a billion to build, and the whispers that the ultraconservative, evangelical Green family, of Hobby Lobby fame, were rumored to be preparing an enormous visitor-conversion machine (rumors of which proved overblown, as the museum experience is designed to appeal to a variety of religious beliefs and, thankfully, aims for objectivity). It was actually a talk given at the annual academic conference on art crime run by the research group I founded, ARCA. The paper was given by Roberta Mazza. In it, she highlighted some concerns about how the Green family was collecting the enormous quantity of biblical artifacts. She showed slides of purchased objects appearing on eBay and sold by pseudonymous sellers with alleged links to looting and possibly even terrorism. She also showed videos of the previous director, before Trobisch took over, dismantling mummies in order to access biblical texts that were written on the papyrus in which they were wrapped—a practice very much frowned upon by most scholars.

Mazza began to look into the Green collection when researching fragments of a recently discovered papyrus by the ancient Greek poet Sappho. "I started searching information about [the collection] through the Internet, and I discovered many details on the acquisition methods, and also on the ignorance in papyrology and conservation care of papyri shown by the ex-director of the collection, Scott Carroll. This man was able to buy about one thousand papyri for Mr. Green from 2009 to 2012." But Carroll was known for finding papyri for collectors—prior to the Greens, he worked for another Christian fundamentalist, Robert van Kampen, and acquired some five thousand papyri for his collection. "I found, and still find, it odd that so many papyri were available on the market in such a short period of time, and maybe by coincidence during the Arab spring. How was he able to find first five thousand papyri and then another [approximately] one thousand [for the Greens] in such a brief period of time, and in the context, in theory, of a strictly regulated antiquities market? Is it possible that, in the past decade, there were at least six thousand papyri which, having legally left Egypt before 1972 (the year of the enforcement of the UNESCO Convention), were sold by their owners?" The numbers are staggering. The UNESCO Convention controls the export of antiquities and makes it bureaucratically difficult to legally sell abroad objects that were excavated after 1972. The idea that thousands of papyri could be on the market means that private collectors with artifacts acquired prior to the 1970s had suddenly decided to sell them and flood the market—or that the papyri had been procured in a possibly illegal manner. Mazza continues, "I have been reassured by Trobisch that all acquisition documents are clear, but I am a scholar, so I need solid proof to be convinced. So far I have not seen any, while the videos and interviews [with Carroll] I saw and read were very worrying." Many of these videos have been taken off YouTube, but Mazza showed some at the ARCA Conference on the Study of Art Crime in 2014 in Amelia. Carroll was shown handling ancient papyri and other artifacts in what appeared to be a manner that ranged from sloppy and haphazard to intentionally destructive. In one video, Carroll explains to a group of students how they will dismantle an ancient mummy mask, before dissolving it in Palmolive soap, pulling the cartonnage apart with toothbrushes, and laying out the strips of cartonnage to examine the text that they contain—a video that led Mazza to dub Carroll "the Palmolive Indiana Jones." Mazza continues: "It suffices to watch Scott Carroll videos, read his interviews and tweets, to be concerned about both his acquisition methods and his questionable practice of destroying mummy masks, with the help of scholars and students of the Green Scholars Initiative, in order to retrieve texts." Harvesting mummy cartonnage is not illegal (provided you are the legitimate owner of the object and it was not excavated or exported illegally) but a question of ethics. As Mazza said, accepting this behavior "allows owners of antiquities legally acquired to dispose of their objects as they wish, even to destroy them," and she wonders whether some new legislation should be implemented that would hinder legal owners from destroying cultural heritage, even if they did acquire it legally. There is a parallel in the world of rare books and prints. A dealer might buy a book containing dozens of antique prints, and then "chop" or "break" the book into pieces, harvesting the prints which can be framed and sold individually, thereby making a profit far greater than the price of the intact book. This is not illegal but is heartbreaking to bibliophiles. If someone bought a Picasso and sliced it into strips, selling each one to a different buyer, then the world would be up in arms. Why isn't this the case with an ancient mummy?

At the annual ARCA conference, and published subsequently in her blog, *Faces and Voices*, Mazza described another problematic papyrus, which contains Coptic text from Galatians 2. When visiting the Green exhibit at the Vatican, Mazza recognized that the Galatians 2 fragment "had, in fact, been put on sale on eBay in 2012 by a much-discussed Turkish account, MixAntik." When Mazza asked Trobisch about the origins of the fragment, she claims that he refuted her suggestion that it had been bought over eBay. But images and a description that match the fragment were indeed on eBay. These were the concerns Mazza addressed at the conference, which made me interested in the whole affair. But I was also intrigued that Trobisch attended the conference, as an audience member (and not by invitation), to hear what Mazza had to say—a very professional move, and one that suggests a clean conscience. That's what drew me to focus on Trobisch, who is not an evangelical but a theologian with an impeccable pedigree.

I came away from research for that article thoroughly impressed with Trobisch, who green-lit (excuse the pun) the item-by-item investigation of the colossal collection, the reins of which were newly in his hands. I was still concerned about the accusations from respected scholars like Mazza, and they had not yet been answered.

Turns out she was right. An investigation by the FBI, begun in October 2015, concluded in 2017. The results are not particularly surprising, considering the fact that the sighting of smoke usually indicates a fire. Federal prosecutors announced July 5 that the Hobby Lobby Stores (not the Green family personally, it should be noted) have agreed to pay a fine of $3 million and to "forfeit thousands of ancient Iraqi artifacts smuggled from the Middle East that the government alleges were intentionally mislabeled," according to the *Post*. This was linked to a bulk purchase of around 5,500 objects, in December 2010, for a price of $1.6 million, many of which were shipped from the Middle East to the United States in ways that suggested smuggling and customs evasion, including labeling contents as "ceramic tiles" and shipping to a variety of addresses, to avoid suspicion that would come from mass shipments to a single one. A single shipment of one thousand clay bullae was shipped, in September 2011, by an Israeli dealer with a fake customs declaration stating that the package came from Israel, when it did not. A United Arab Emirates dealer shipped packages with fake documentation that they were coming from Turkey. The federal investigators were concerned that these artifacts were coming from illicit archaeological sites, were looted or stolen, and were emerging from conflict zones, like Iraq. It appears that these fears were justified. In the worst-case scenarios, some of these purchases may even be funding terrorist activity, which is not in the least unlikely, given their origins and the knowledge that fundamentalist terrorist groups fund their activities through antiquities looting.

New "Intelligence" Body Will Monitor Illegal Traffic in Cultural Property

The International Council of Museums (ICOM) announced the foundation of an "Intelligence" body to monitor illegal traffic in cultural property.

This new group will be called the International Observatory on Illicit Traffic in Cultural Goods. It will work as a bridge between UNESCO, Interpol, and its constituent policing agencies, as well as other research institutions in the field. The "Observatory" is now awaiting formal funding approval from the European Commission.

The story of this group was first broken by Ian Johnston of *NBC News*. An ICOM official who spoke to Mr. Johnston, but asked not to be named, discussed how traffic in cultural property is "much worse than other types of theft." The contact went on: "ICOM felt it needed a lot more reliable information and recent analyses of trends, what one would call the need for 'intelligence' when fighting organized criminal activity."

It has long been known that art crime is a funding source for organized crime, from small local gangs to large international syndicates, but the true extent remains uncertain. Until the US Department of Justice recently remade their website, they stated clearly that art crime is the third-highest-grossing criminal trade worldwide, behind only the drug and arms trades, and that it is a major funding source for organized crime and even terrorism (the new website design no longer has a page dedicated to cultural property crimes). Interpol has, in the past, reiterated this information, but currently states that while experts have made such claims, it simply does not have enough information to confirm or deny them.

This brings up an oft-asked question: Where do these statistics come from?

An official who prefers not to be named, but has strong connections to the relevant agencies, explained: "This information comes from the UK National Threat Assessment, conducted by SOCA (the United Kingdom's Serious Organized Crime Agency). The statistics were provided by Scotland Yard, but are classified. The report containing this information was submitted in 2006–2007 and it remained in the Threat Assessment for several years. The terrorist links to the Middle East come from the Interpol Tracking Task Force in Iraq and were reported at the annual Interpol Stolen Works of Art meeting in Lyon in 2008 and 2009, after prior meetings were held in Lyon, Amman, and Washington. The head of Interpol Baghdad claimed to have proof of the link between Islamic fundamentalist terrorist groups and art crime (primarily antiquities looting). All of the major players, from Interpol to the US Department of Justice, believed the reports and still broadcast the claims of it, so there is no reason to doubt it—but the details are likely still classified."

This sort of response may be frustrating to those who want specifics, but it does explain both where the oft-quoted data comes from, and why we don't know much beyond the broad-stroke headlines. The aforementioned investigation followed a 2004 article in the German magazine *Der Spiegel* that broke an unknown element to the story of Mohammed Atta, one of the organizers of the September 11 attack. Atta had flown to Germany in 1999 to try to sell looted Afghani antiquities. When asked why he wanted to sell them, he said that he wanted to buy a plane. It seems that an early iteration of the September 11 attack would have used funds generated from selling looted antiquities to buy planes to crash into buildings. Because investigations of terrorist activity often remain classified, it is understandable that investigations of terrorist-related funding sources, including looted antiquities, would remain likewise. One thing is clear, however: it is not just the art that is at stake.

We know distressingly little about art crime, because it has largely been sidelined as a field of study, due to the mistaken impression that it consists merely of a handful of cinematic museum heists each year, like the recent Rotterdam heist (2012). In actuality, there are tens of thousands of artworks reported stolen each year (twenty to thirty thousand in Italy alone) and far more go unreported. Police recovery rates for stolen art are not encouraging—some studies have suggested that they are as low as 1.5 percent, and at best around 10 percent of what is reported stolen is recovered. Few countries have any dedicated art police, because the general public and authorities alike seem unaware of the severity of art crime, its connections to the drug and arms trades, or have not been given access to enough of the data to determine for themselves if funds should really be dedicated to policing stolen art.

How do criminals profit from stolen art? Some art is stolen for ransom, and some works are sold, although there is no known market for recognizable stolen art. Looted antiquities, on the other hand, of the sort on which ICOM's new International Observatory on Illicit Traffic in Cultural Goods will focus, are taken directly from the earth (or the sea) and therefore have never existed before to modern humans. They will never appear on a stolen art registry and can be sold openly, often for full value, accompanied only by forged provenance that suggests the objects were legally excavated and exported. Because of the interplay between drugs, arms, and art among organized crime groups of varying sizes, there are other ways to benefit from stolen art, beyond selling it.

When I taught a seminar in art crime at Yale in 2009, a local thief provided a useful case study. Dennis Maluk was a heroin addict, living in New Haven. He stole at least thirty-nine paintings from the greater New Haven area, nothing famous but some of them worth thousands of dollars. He traded each of them to Bruno Nestir, a local member of a criminal gang, in exchange for a day or two's worth of heroin. When police raided Nestir's home, they found thirty-nine stolen paintings, drugs packaged for street sale, unlicensed firearms, and a wad of cash. There, in miniature, we see what can happen to stolen art when even small, local criminal gangs are involved.

A larger-scale case study may be found in the 1986 theft of art from Russborough House, a country house in Ireland which has the unusual distinction of having been burgled of its art on four separate occasions, twice by the IRA. This time it was Martin Cahill, an infamous Irish gangster about whom films have been made. He and accomplices stole eighteen works from Russborough House, including a Vermeer, a Goya, and a Gabriël Metsu. He figured that he would retire on the proceeds, but Cahill could not find the sort of criminal art collector he expected from books and the movies. Unable to find a buyer who did not look like a policeman in disguise, he hatched another plan. He smuggled the Vermeer and the Goya to Antwerp, where he used them as collateral for a loan of one million pounds from a diamond merchant who had bought stolen gems from him in the past. The idea was that the loan would go to buying drugs which would be sold on the street for profit. Cahill would pay back the loan, and retrieve the paintings, which would go on to act as collateral in future such deals. That was what was supposed to happen, but the diamond merchant got antsy. He decided to sell the paintings himself, and he did—to a Scotland Yard undercover agent, who arrested him. A different work also stolen by Cahill, the Gabriël Metsu, was recovered when police in Istanbul raided a deal between two organized crime groups, trading the Metsu for a shipment of drugs. In the Cahill case, we see stolen art used as collateral and in a barter system between criminal groups.

The interconnection between drugs, arms, and stolen art is serious. Art theft might be fun and sexy to read about, but if you are concerned about the drug and arms trade, and even terrorism, then it is something to take seriously. Hopefully, this new International Observatory on Illicit Traffic in Cultural Goods will prompt more accessible and extensive data and better cooperation to both protect the world's cultural heritage and simultaneously impede organized crime.

Oops or Illegal? What Happens When Two Artists Have the Same Idea?

The talk of the 2017 Venice Biennale was not the brilliant idea of a great artist, but rather the brilliant idea of two great artists . . . who happened to have had the exact same idea. It's an awkward sort of moment, like when two Hollywood starlets show up on the red carpet wearing the exact same glamorous ball gown that each thought was a unique, bespoke piece of couture. But the question on everyone's mind, once the awkwardness passed, was whether anything illegal or immoral had taken place. Had one of the artists stolen the idea from the other? Or was this just a monumentally weird coincidence?

The drama was heightened by the fact that both of the artists are renowned, but one is arguably the most famous artist alive and is in a close race for the title of the highest-earning artist in history: Damien Hirst. The naughty imp of the contemporary British art scene is known for a dark and incubus-like sense of humor. If there were any artist who might pull some sort of stunt like this on purpose, he seemed like a good candidate. But the reaction of his camp suggests nothing of the sort. There was genuine concern and official statements from lawyers and nothing particularly fun or funny about it.

The problem is this: both Hirst and the artist presenting at the Grenada Pavilion, Jason deCaires Taylor, presented installations at the Biennale which were meant to look like ancient sculptures that had been lodged for centuries at the bottom of the ocean, after a shipwreck or natural disaster, and which were recently salvaged but not cleaned. Thus we have naturalistic life-size statues of humans covered in various oceanic growth, coral, and debris. Both are accompanied by murky underwater photographs of the statues in situ, underwater where they were "discovered." In Hirst's case, these photos are staged, as the sculptures were never actually underwater. In the case of deCaires Taylor, his shtick as an artist is to actually sink new sculptures into the sea and allow them to be partially swallowed up by the undersea world, then to photograph them. I know, weird "coincidence," right?

Hirst's installation is entitled *Treasures from the Wreck of the Unbelievable* while deCaires Taylor's is called *The Bridge*. Anyone who sees both shows, or reads about both shows, logically asks: Well, who thought of it first, and did whoever come up with it second steal the idea from the first guy? A fair enough question, but a complicated one to answer.

Art sometimes, but not always, emerges with a "eureka moment" or is made all in one go. But just as often ideas gestate for years, sketches are made, concepts toyed with, works partly created then set aside, and so on, piecemeal. DeCaires Taylor is pretty much the go-to guy when it comes to underwater sculpture installations, the first artist to take on the Land Art movement, which is associated with human-made (or human-arranged) terrestrial installations that artists permit nature to engage with, and erode, as they see fit. In 2006, he set up the world's first underwater sculpture garden, which visitors can admire by snorkel or scuba, in the sea beside the island of Grenada. So it is reasonable of him to feel that this is his territory, and that it has been encroached upon. For his part, deCaires Taylor has taken the high road and issued a statement that is just about devoid of hard feelings, saying, "After viewing Hirst's latest exhibition, it seems I have certainly created an art genre that has been responded to." He goes on to say that the message behind his art is very different from Hirst's. He tries to send environmental messages, and the main sculptures in his Biennale show, entitled *Bleached I* and *Bleached II*, refer to "coral bleaching," a damaging byproduct of global warming.

Hirst, on the other hand, is in it for the fun and the spectacle. Being a big enough gun to speak through spokespeople, a statement was issued on his behalf saying, "Damien has always been fascinated by what he describes as 'the action of the world on things' and he became interested in coralized works in the late nineties, when he sunk some objects off the coast of Mexico." Both artists can claim to have been into sinking sculptures underwater for decades. The art looks different, even if the broad-stroke concepts are strikingly similar. So there is no question of direct replicas or forgeries.

But did one person steal the other's intellectual property? Can the concept of a work of art be protected? You certainly could not claim intellectual property theft when more than one artist thought to sculpt the execution of the first-century Jewish *tekton* who thought he was the Messiah. There are a good deal more crucifixes around the world than you could shake many sticks at, and though the concept and subject matter are extremely specific, no one is suing anyone else for making crucifixion sculptures.

When in doubt as to a legal matter in the art world, I turn to Edgar Tijhuis, an Amsterdam-based art crime specialist and lawyer. On this issue, he said, "It is definitely a rare coincidence that potentially raises questions about intellectual property. But it is doubtful whether there is any objective legal basis for action on the side of Jason deCaires Taylor against Damien Hirst, especially since Taylor himself stressed the differences between their respective works and Hirst claimed (through a spokesperson) to have been interested in this kind of work since the late 1990s." Unless some document surfaced that overtly demonstrated otherwise, this will remain just a coincidence, even if a suspicious one, and not an idea theft that could be proven in court.

It is interesting that no one seems worried that deCaires Taylor got the idea from Hirst. It has been his calling card as an artist, whereas Hirst dips into this and that, with that middle finger–wielding naughty prankster attitude being the most consistent element in his oeuvre. Hirst is also one of the richest artists ever to have lived and has a vast staff promoting and protecting him, so he's the one who feels vulnerable to attack. This was evident from his reticence, allowing a spokesperson to make a statement for him, whereas deCaires Taylor was being jokey on social media and appeared the one with nothing to hide.

Ideas float (or in this case, perhaps sink), and the history of art is largely populated with a relatively small number of concepts and scenes that artists use and reuse, repeat and reinterpret, ad infinitum. This had to do with the textual inspirations for most historical Western art (the Bible, the Golden Legend, pagan mythology, Ovid, true history) and the limited scope of imagination of most commissioners of older Western art, who liked to patronize religious art and portraits of themselves and their families. A visual lexicon of just a few hundred subjects fills a good 80 percent or more of Western art history books. Overlap is part of the game.

That in mind, perhaps the best we can take out of this is to look at the two shows side by side and determine which we deem most successful. The ideas are the same, but what of the execution and the refinement, the use of the general concept? In a courtroom, there would be no winner in this case. But gallery versus gallery, show versus show, who did a better job with the raw conceptual material, transmuting it into tangible art? That's up to you.

The Getty Set to Lose Its Bronze

According to Pliny, the Athenian sculptor Lysippus made around 1,500 works during his career, all of them in bronze. Though many marble Roman copies after his lost originals exist, only one original is thought to survive: the so-called *Victorious Youth*, also known as the *Getty Bronze*, displayed in the J. Paul Getty Museum in California.

But that unique statue by the most celebrated sculptor of the ancient world was very likely looted and acquired inappropriately by the Getty.

On June 8, 2018, Italian magistrate Giacomo Gasparini published a decision about the *Getty Bronze*, as first reported in English on the blog of ARCA, the Association for Research into Crimes against Art, which had been purchased by the museum in 1977 for $3.95 million.

The Getty claimed that there was no evidence that the statue was looted from Italy, contesting the allegations of the Italian advocate general and Ministry of Culture. Italy brought the argument to trial, requesting the repatriation of the statue on the grounds that it illegally left Italy, where it had been discovered.

This case was far less cut-and-dried than other Getty-related art looting scandals, of which unfortunately there have been many, and they have been much publicized, as evident in a *Guardian* newspaper headline: "Getty Museum admits 350 more treasures may be looted" (and that was back in 2006, before other allegations came to light). In this case, the Getty consistently argued that Italy should have no claim to this statue, which was made by an Athenian and supposedly found in international waters in 1964, having survived thanks to the "good fortune" of having been sunken in a shipwreck (most of the bronzes of the ancient world that were on land were melted down and reused, so those that were lost in shipwrecks were more likely to be preserved, as outlined in *The Museum of Lost Art*). The question of who "owns" such an object is complex, but Italy argues that the statue, which was brought to shore at the coastal town of Fano, was subsequently illegally exported from Italy. The story goes that the fishermen aboard a boat called the *Ferruccio Feri* smuggled the statue into town, to avoid having to declare it to their own, Italian customs authorities. As the ARCA blog described it, they "hid it from authorities, first by burying it in a cabbage patch and later by hiding it in a priest's bathtub."

The Getty's attorney argued in court that John Paul Getty himself had refused to buy the statue. Their Italian counterparts said that his refusal was because he must have known that it was an illegal offering. But the Getty attorneys said that this was not the reason—J. Paul Getty was rather distracted at the time, because his sixteen-year-old grandson, John Paul Getty III, had been kidnapped while in Rome in 1973. The legal path leading to this decision is labyrinthine, to say the least, with multiple courts at multiple levels, dating back nearly ten years, ruling that the statue was illegally exported, with the Getty appealing each time, and the case bouncing up to ever-higher courts.

Now the case at its current judicial level has finally concluded. The judge rejected the Getty's opposition to Italy's proposed confiscation of the statue. That means that, legally, Italy has the right to confiscate the statue and bring it back "home." Exactly when it will be seized is now the question, or perhaps Italy and the Getty will reach some agreement, as has been the case in some past instances in which objects (unfortunately several from the Getty, which has a problematic acquisition history) have been identified as having been illegally excavated and/or exported from Italy.

The Getty released a statement saying that it is "reviewing the decision," which the museum found "disappointing." They reiterated the argument that the statue was found in "international waters" and in 1964, which is a key date–it is prior to the 1970 UNESCO Convention, which greatly tightened international laws on legal excavation and export of cultural heritage. Prior to 1970, nations had varied laws that were irregularly enforced. Courts have granted a sort of an amnesty to objects that were exported prior to 1970–more specifically, it is far more difficult to prove illegal exportation in cases prior to 1970 than those after. As a result, some questionable objects have been assigned exportation dates (in some cases fraudulently) prior to 1970, in order to make them more difficult to seize. This is not necessarily the case here, but there are precedents for it, and so the precise exportation date comes into scrutiny.

The larger problem is that the Getty has long been infamous for acquiring illegal pieces, as has been covered at length in all manner of newspapers and in books like *Chasing Aphrodite*, *The Lost Chalice*, and *I Predatori dell'Arte Perduta*. Getty curators have been convicted in Italian courts of having knowingly purchased looted antiquities, as in the case of Marion True, and internal memos have come to light suggesting that the Getty administration was aware that objects they wished to acquire were problematic, but that they should acquire them anyway. In 2006, for instance, the Getty agreed to return twenty-six objects to Italy, twenty-five of which were claimed by the Italian Ministry of Culture after careful detective work by the Office of the Advocate General, particularly archaeologist Stefano Alessandrini.

The Getty has repeatedly been found to have acquired illegal objects, has defended itself, and has been obliged to return objects. This Lysippus statue is just the latest in a long line of unfortunate issues at the world's richest museum. (Note: this ruling was upheld in 2024 and the Lysippus will finally go back to Italy.)

The Google Loot Project

An attempt to smuggle an ancient carved stone into Britain was foiled by a Google search. The customs officer on duty thought it was suspicious that the smuggler was bearing a "carved stone for home decoration" valued at "300," as was written on the customs declaration. Indeed, it is a carved stone, but it turned out to be an extremely rare and valuable Babylonian kudurru, an official document recording a gift of property made by the king. A Google search by the customs officer led to him contacting the British Museum, which confirmed what the object was, and its great value. It will be returned to Iraq shortly.

TEFAF Maastricht is the premiere venue for selling Old Master artworks, and as with most fairs of its type (from Art Basel to the Armory Show to Olympia and beyond), the fair organizers do their due diligence to minimize the risk that an object on sale is problematic (read as: looted, stolen, or a forgery). But there are inevitable slips through the cracks.

A British Museum curator was quoted in the *Guardian* as saying, "This kudurru has been neither previously recorded nor published, and must therefore come from illicit digging." That is a very important point that trends against how the art trade tends to behave. A lack of provenance may be taken as a red flag for conscientious collectors and dealers, but too often it is considered par for the course. The rationalization goes something like this: just because there is no provenance does not mean that the object is illicit. This can be true, because objects do not come with folders full of documents. Curators, dealers, auction houses, scholars, and researchers must set off on archival treasure hunts to figure out the story of objects based on little or no additional knowledge beyond the object itself. So, the thinking goes, there is surely a documented history to this object, it just has not yet been unearthed. In short: any good object that can be sold should be sold, unless there is empirical evidence showing that it must not be sold. The British Museum curator's point went the other way around: unless one can find documented evidence that the piece is legitimate, we must presume that it is not.

It's easy to see how one argument gives benefit of the doubt to legitimacy and favors the market, while the other seeks to protect against looting and traffic in cultural heritage. This is always likely to be a case of trade versus scholars. So how do art fairs and galleries avoid being liable should they inadvertently (or, in rare cases, advertently) sell a looted or stolen object?

They must prove due diligence, a legal term that indicates that they checked to ensure that the object in question was not overtly illicit. To do this, they will check their offerings against stolen art databases. There are many, all of them private. Larger companies will pay firms to check against their respective, private databases. One of them has around half a million stolen objects on file, which sounds like a lot, but Italy's Carabinieri Division for the Protection of Cultural Heritage runs its own database, nicknamed Leonardo, that has over five million—by far the world's largest. The FBI, by contrast, has only a few thousand objects on their database. Interpol, which gathers data from its 125 member countries, had just forty-one thousand objects in their stolen works of art database (as of 2013).

There are some problems with this current default method of covering due diligence. First is that checking an object, say a Babylonian kudurru, against the database and not finding a match does not mean that the object is legitimate and was not looted or stolen. It simply means that, of the X number of items in the database in question, there was no match. Or the software did not find one (for objects are sometimes altered to evade such image-recognition software). However, failure to find a match on a database check is enough for the trade to consider that they've done their part, and can go ahead and sell the object. Cultural heritage illegally excavated, fresh from the earth, will of course never appear on a database, because it will not have been seen by modern humans. Databases are good at covering objects registered in collections, stolen, and then registered as having been stolen with the police, but not very helpful with anything else.

But they could be, and this brings me to two modest proposals, both of which are discussed among students every year at the ARCA Postgraduate Program in Art Crime and Cultural Heritage Protection but for the time being remain solely in the realm of theory. The first is that the divisive nature of many different, private, imperfect databases (sometimes run by rival organizations) is inherently problematic.

A single, universal database would be best for all, but the nature of ego and bureaucracy means this is unlikely to happen. Making such a database public, available not just through specialized firms or to law enforcement but to dealers and, most importantly, potential buyers of such art, would be a democratizing step in the right direction. A sort of "Google Loot Project," in which you could photograph an object for sale with your phone and receive a message as to whether it is likely to be problematic. But even this is still imperfect, because as stated, not finding a match is no guarantee that the object is legit. The software must be flexible enough to flag objects of the sort known to have been looted. There was never going to be a match for the Babylonian kudurru, unless it was stolen from a collection—if it was illegally excavated, no search would come up with it. One must recognize that objects from conflict zones are problematic, hence the categories of objects featured on the International Council of Museums (ICOM) "red lists," in which types of objects known to be circulating illegally from various at-risk countries are indicated.

There is one further step, and it is the best way to curb looting and the various bad things it often funds, from organized crime to terrorism. It has already been stated by the British Museum curator, but it bears repeating. If the trade were to agree that, unless there is overt evidence found that an object was legally excavated, exported, and is not stolen then it cannot be sold, then the vast majority of art crime would run into a wall. But this would reduce the bottom line, and without strong and international legislation backing it up, it's unlikely to happen. So perhaps the Google Loot Project idea is more feasible—unify the stolen art databases and justify them with the likes of ICOM's red lists, so that types of objects, not just direct matches, will be flagged. Make it easier for everyone to check to see if cultural heritage is likely legitimate, therefore making it tougher to claim that you were fooled if you go ahead and deal in or acquire a problematic object. The Latin term *caveat emptor*, "buyer beware," is most often used as a warning against purchasing forgeries, but it is just as applicable here, where the market is scattered with looted and stolen goods that the market's current defenses are not sufficient to protect against.

Do NFTs Mean the End of Real-World Art?

We just witnessed what may be the first theft in the history of art crime that involves addition without subtraction. There have been thefts in which works were swapped. In 2014, Matisse's *Odalisque in Red Trousers* was recovered, after an FBI sting operation, and returned to the Caracas Museum of Contemporary Art in Venezuela, from which it had been stolen. Yet it took two years for anyone to notice that the painting had been stolen. The real Matisse had been taken back in 2000, but no one was aware of the theft until 2002, because the thieves had swapped a very good forgery in its place. But that was a swap. How about stealing by only adding?

What we witnessed is a case in which the illusion of adding an artwork could have resulted in the value of other artwork lowering by tens of millions.

The example I'm referring to happened on April 4, 2021, and involved a hack of the artist Beeple, whose claim to fame is having created and minted an NFT (nonfungible token), *Everydays: The First 5000 Days*, which was sold at Christie's for $69 million, making it one of the most expensive artworks in history. The value of this, as with the value of all art (digital or otherwise) is in a combination of its perceived rarity plus perceived demand plus perceived authenticity. Because there's only one original *Everydays: The First 5000 Days* (the file is huge, so the images available online are a miniature thumbnail derivative for promotion only) it has value.

But if they were two, then suddenly the value would be significantly less—tens of millions less. While Beeple was the one hacked, it was MetaKovan, the buyer of the original, who was almost "robbed" not of the NFT itself but of its perceived value. This was the trick being pulled by a hacker who calls himself Monsieur Personne (French for Mister Nobody) and who said that his goal was "not out of malice" but merely to point out the silliness he or she sees in the NFT craze. He did so by "sleepminting," or registering a new NFT as if it came from an artist. It was as if Beeple woke one morning to see a forgery of a Beeple sitting in his studio on the easel. The "thief" (if we can even call him that) has minted the term "sleepminting" and launched a website, NFTheft. It is all a publicity stunt but one can see how money could be earned falsely. And if the truth had not been outed so swiftly, MetaKovan and his $69 million NFT might have been robbed of most of its value.

We are entering what experts call a mega cycle of NFTs. Nonfungible tokens are like cryptocurrency (Bitcoin and the like) but cannot be directly cashed out. Instead they are a way of linking a file (a jpeg, an mp3) to blockchain to demonstrate its authenticity and rarity. NFTs have been all over the news over the last year, so much so that I'm writing a book about them and their relationship to the art trade. They may seem like just the latest overhyped trend. And it is easy to see it from that perspective, but I see it differently. To me, they're just the latest incarnation of using technology to create art.

In the 1980s, when video art was introduced, many thought that it was a silly trend that would never last. How, they wondered, can you give value to something that can be copied from VHS to VHS? The answer was that there were one or more originals (a unique "mother" VHS of the video artwork or a limited series endorsed by the artist). The system worked and endured. Going back still further, some wondered, circa 1500, how prints by master artists like Albrecht Dürer could have value if they were produced in a mechanical printing press and existed in extensive series. But they retained value and still do because of perceived rarity, demand, and authenticity.

NFTs look set to last not only for this reason, but because they have a number of advantages that will help them endure. One is the ability for artists to release their work directly. That has not quite happened yet; at the moment you still need a platform. But basically, the platform is a way to announce to the world that you have a new product, as is the case with OpenSea, which seems to be the most popular for proper artists. It functions much like an online art gallery, but with fees far lower than the 50 percent art galleries usually take.

There is also the immediacy of delivery and absence of significant costs for transport and handling and insurance. The downside of this is that the only way to look at your art or display it is in virtual online galleries, like those in Decentraland, a website comprised of a virtual world where virtual versions of users can explore virtual collectibles that they bought with virtual currency.

Yes, we've entered the Matrix. But one imagines that it is just a matter of time before technology will catch up and make enjoying your NFTs as easy as it is to collect them. Crypto wallets will likely have art gallery features in the future, and there will be the ability to loan your digital unique image to galleries and screens the world over—MetaKovan has talked about loaning his Beeple NFT, for instance. I recently curated a virtual exhibition, *Missing Masterpieces*, that was visible only on Samsung Frame televisions, and a digital screen like that is ideally suited to present a collection of NFTs.

Another advantage is that, theoretically, blockchain technology makes NFTs immune to theft or forgery. The promise of blockchain technology is really just digital provenance. Provenance describes the documented history of an object, its ownership, where it was displayed and so on. Blockchain technology simply takes this and digitizes it in immutable code that cannot be altered or erased but only added to. This means that there can never be any doubt as to whether someone who is in possession of an NFT is actually the owner, or whether that NFT is original or not, because the blockchain provenance will trace it back to its creator.

Yet, for every brilliant technological innovation, there is someone with too much brain, and a bit too much time on their hands, who will come up with a way to defeat it. This was made evident by Monsieur Personne, whose quite ingenious action was merely a way to show that the emperor has no clothes. The "sleepminting" hack was sufficiently skillful that it seemed that this new NFT had indeed come from Beeple himself. This was quickly set right and there was no harm done. It may even be considered an artistic action in the form of illegal activity, along the lines of Ulay's *Irritation: There's a Criminal Touch to Art.*

In the end, the NFTheft, as Monsieur Personne calls it, actually publicized NFTs more than undermined them and perhaps even underscored their relevance, because if something is worth hacking, then it is worthy of attention. But it does show that even foolproof technology sets a bar that some people will try to leap over, or crawl under.

NFTs do not spell the end of IRL art (that's short for "In Real Life"—don't worry, I had to look it up, too). They are simply a new chapter. Artists are now racing to create their own NFTs, as most of what exists now is mediocre and uninteresting, from an art perspective. And yet people are throwing money at it. Banksy has created them. Only now Damien Hirst has announced that he will, too. Others follow suit. The European conceptual artist JAŠA released *The Monuments Fragments*, which allows patrons to buy NFTs and, in doing so, fund the construction of an architectural space in which durational performances will take place (JAŠA's best-known project, *Utter*, at the 2015 Venice Biennale had a similar format). Those NFTs also function as tickets for the patrons to attend the performances, which are otherwise closed to the public. Patrons can also print and frame the NFT images, thereby making an IRL artwork out of a digital one—the opposite of what we're used to, in taking a digital photo of a physically existing artwork. Then the sixteen fragments available, once sold, will form together, like Voltron, into a Monuments Mother Image, a new NFT, which will likewise be available for purchase. The possibilities are endless.

Now that we have proper artists, entering the fray, we are just at the start of a long extension of the mega cycle. NFTs should indeed be considered a new art format, one that is in its nascent years, or rather, with the speed of the digital world, its nascent weeks. It is not so different from video art or other technological leaps forward that left many people scratching their heads. NFTs' value is directly parallel to why art has always been valued. My prediction is that the tsunami of uninteresting NFTs will cool and recede, but now that proper artists and creators are entering the fray, the collecting of blockchain-provenanced, digital-first (and often -only) artworks will endure and thrive.

3 ART, CRIME, AND POPULAR CULTURE

When Picasso Stole the *Mona Lisa*: A Belgian Art Thief, Two Red Herrings, and the *Affaire des Statuettes*

On August 21, 1911, Leonardo's *Mona Lisa*—the world's most famous artwork—was stolen from the Louvre Museum. The thief was Vincenzo Peruggia, an Italian handyman and amateur painter. But police would not learn this for years. For lack of leads, they followed anything that seemed promising. Then someone with a known connection to the Polish-born poet Guillaume Apollinaire and his best friend, Spanish-born painter Pablo Picasso, wrote to a Parisian newspaper. He complained that he had planned to steal the *Mona Lisa* and whoever had taken the painting had messed up his system, by which he had been regularly stealing from the Louvre. Police leapt at the chance. They brought in first Apollinaire, then Picasso for questioning. The two were entirely innocent of the *Mona Lisa* theft, but were terrified because they were guilty of having been involved in stealing other things from the Louvre. (For more on the *Mona Lisa*, see my book *The Thefts of the* Mona Lisa: *The Complete Story of the World's Most Famous Painting*.)

The so-called *affaire des statuettes* is surprisingly little known, despite having been confirmed on all sides, including in the memoir of Picasso's lover at the time, Fernande Olivier, and by Picasso himself. I'm a professor specializing in the history of art crime, and the general rule is that criminal collectors of art do not exist outside the realm of film and fiction. Collectors who commission the theft of artworks they desire can be counted in the low dozens (a miniscule number when we consider that tens of thousands of artworks are reported stolen each year, as many as twenty thousand a year in Italy alone). But Picasso is among them. My research into the *affaire des statuettes* makes clear that Picasso was knowingly involved in stealing several ancient Iberian statue heads from the Louvre Museum, probably not only commissioning the theft but also participating in it. And the theft proved integral to the creation of Picasso's first masterpiece, *Les Demoiselles d'Avignon*, often called the first modernist artwork.

The main thief, and the man who wrote to a Parisian newspaper complaining about the *Mona Lisa* theft having disrupted his own burgling, was a Belgian con man, secretary, soldier, and later a cowboy, by the name of Honoré Joseph Géry-Pieret. He had been working, circa 1907, as a personal secretary for Apollinaire, a renowned journalist, modern art critic, and poet. Géry-Pieret was also a compulsive art thief. He stole from the Louvre so often that he once asked his girlfriend, Marie Laurencin, "Marie, I'm off to the Louvre this afternoon. Can I bring you anything you need?" She thought he meant something from the shopping arcade adjacent to the Louvre, when he meant the museum itself.

By his own admission, Géry-Pieret began stealing from the Louvre in March 1907, though evidence suggests that he began some time earlier. An Iberian statue head was stolen in November 1906, and the theft was featured in the newspaper *Le Matin*. That article mentions the low financial value of Iberian statue heads in general, stating that the thief might be "a possessive and discreet collector who has no interest in money, but keeps [the statues] in the most secret part of his apartment getting drunk on their beauty in solitude." That a criminal collector must be behind art thefts is a suggestion that the media regularly touted, though there are very few known historical instances of it being the case. This would prove to be one of those very few exceptions.

In his letter, sent after the *Mona Lisa* had been stolen and had captured the headlines, Géry-Pieret boasted of having smuggled the statue heads out of the museum under his coat, stopping en route to ask a museum guard for directions to the nearest exit. He was clearly interested in touting his accomplishments, perhaps with unrealistic grace notes embellishing the true story. In agreement with *Paris-Journal*, the thief Géry-Pieret committed to writing his story, which they published in the same August 29 edition of their newspaper.

The flush of press brought on first by the *Mona Lisa* theft and now by the uproar caused by the publication of Géry-Pieret's letters frightened Picasso and Apollinaire. Gery-Pieret's version of the story saw him as the sole thief. But the work of a modern scholar, Silvia Loreti, found that there were holes in it. The statue heads were too cumbersome for one person to easily carry, much less under their coat. And the heads, which had been on display when Picasso first saw them and fell in love with them—seeing in them an ancient predecessor to his own, contemporary Iberian art aesthetic—were by 1907 in storage. That means this could not have been a crime of opportunity but had to be well planned, with the thief (or more likely thieves) descending into Louvre storage to fish out exactly the statuettes they were after.

One of the statue heads, which had been stolen in 1911 and returned along with the first letter by Géry-Pieret, had been stashed in Apollinaire's apartment. But the other two statues, those returned by Apollinaire, had been in Picasso's possession since their theft in 1907. We know that Picasso kept them hidden among his clothes because his lover at the time, Fernande Olivier, had noted in her memoir how she always found it odd that, of all of the artworks in Picasso's collection, most of which were displayed prominently around his apartment and studio, only these two statue heads remained resident at the bottom of his wardrobe. She wrote that Picasso "took great care of his [1907] gifts and kept them buried in a wardrobe."

Fernande Olivier wrote of the affair in her memoir: "Géry-Pieret gave Picasso two little statuettes without revealing where he had acquired them. He said only that they should not be displayed in too conspicuous a manner. Picasso was enchanted and he treasured these gifts and buried them at the back of a cupboard." Her memoir continues, explaining how worried Apollinaire and Picasso were, making plans to flee the country. They thought to dispose of the evidence and put the heads in a suitcase, intent on throwing it into the Seine, but came home with the suitcase still in hand.

The pressure was so great that Apollinaire made the dangerous and perhaps foolish decision to personally return the two statue heads that had been stolen in 1907. He left them at the *Paris-Journal* office on September 5, 1911. The next day the newspaper published an article about their return, featuring photographs of the statuettes along with the excuse provided by the unnamed owner: "One would not think that such unrefined objects could have been part of the Louvre collection . . . seduced by the relatively low price, he purchased them."

Seeing their photographs in the paper, Louvre curator Edmond Pottier recognized the two statue heads as entries AM1140 and AM1141 in the Inventory of Mediterranean Antiquities kept by the museum. Pottier immediately contacted the newspaper, and was told that the statues had been brought in by "an honorable individual, who had purchased the two heads for a small amount of money, and who had grown concerned after the rumors in the press about the thefts of the Iberian statuettes, and thinking that he might, without realizing it, have purchased stolen objects, he brought them in to the newspaper."

On September 7, Apollinaire was arrested under several accusations, half of them true. He was accused of harboring the thief of the Iberian statue heads, of which he was guilty. But the Paris police, grasping for a positive headline to offset the lack of progress on the *Mona Lisa* case, threw in another charge that was based on no apparent evidence: that Apollinaire was also involved in the theft of the *Mona Lisa*.

The police needed a scapegoat, and Apollinaire was an ideal choice, in that he appealed to the xenophobia of the French at the time. He was born in 1880 in Rome as Wilhelm Albert Włodzimierz Apolinary Kostrowicki, his mother a member of the minor nobility of Poland. His father was most likely Francesco Flugi d'Aspermont, a Swiss Italian aristocrat who left soon after Apollinaire's birth. Apollinaire grew up speaking French, was educated in Monaco, and lived most of his life in Paris, in love with France and the French language and later considered to be one of the greatest francophone poets. But he was a foreigner and, in a country where the madness of the Dreyfus affair was a fresh memory, he was an ideal scapegoat. Right-wing publications attacked him—his biggest crime from their perspective was not having been born French.

In police custody, Apollinaire vehemently denied involvement in the thefts of either the statue heads or the *Mona Lisa*. He did however admit that he knew the man who had stolen the statue heads. He had housed Honoré Joseph Géry-Pieret during the thefts, employing him as a personal secretary but dismissing him from service soon after the thefts took place. This was how the police first became aware of the name Géry-Pieret, who was quickly recognized as the author of the pseudonymous letters to *Paris-Journal*. Apollinaire was compelled to reveal the link to Picasso in the Louvre theft, which led to Picasso being questioned. The two were interrogated separately, and neither represented himself with honor. Picasso was so frightened, particularly of being deported back to Spain, that he denied having ever seen Apollinaire, at that time his closest friend.

Picasso and Apollinaire were both released. Picasso wound up painting some of the statue heads over the faces of the prostitutes in his *Les Demoiselles d'Avignon*. Géry-Pieret was arrested in Cairo in late 1913 on suspicion of involvement with the *Mona Lisa*, but the courts there acquitted him. "I was glad of this," Apollinaire wrote. "The poor fellow was crazy rather than criminal; the courts must have thought so, too." Géry-Pieret made his way to the United States, where he was last heard of working as a cowboy near San Diego.

After Apollinaire was cleared of involvement in the *Mona Lisa* theft, the air cleared and both he and Picasso were left with a still greater celebrity, albeit for the dubious achievement of having been wrongfully accused of the most famous heist in history, while at the same time being guilty of an only slightly less-objectionable series of thefts from the same museum.

There is a sad coda to Apollinaire's involvement in the *affaire des statuettes*, first noted by Peter Read in his book on the friendship of the Polish poet and Picasso. The affair may have actually led, albeit indirectly, to Apollinaire's tragic, premature death. Apollinaire loved France and was devastated by the xenophobic accusations and attacks against him in 1911. Three years later, fate would present him with an opportunity to prove his loyalty to his adopted country.

At the start of the First World War, Apollinaire volunteered for the French army. He died from influenza while hospitalized for a head wound received in action. He was a part of the third of Europe who lost their lives before the war wound down to a close.

The Iberian statuettes are now back at the Louvre, although not always on display. They played a key role in the history of art, thanks to their cameo in the birth of modernism in Picasso's 1907 *Les Demoiselles d'Avignon*. And they will forever be remembered for the supporting role they played in the story of the theft of the *Mona Lisa*.

Is "Affordable" Art Undesirable?

London hosts an annual "Affordable Art Fair." This has been a staple since 1999, with around a quarter million visitors each year, and parallel fairs in ten cities. The definition of "affordable" is works priced under 2,500 GBP, with some sold for as little as 50. But while the prices are low, the quantity is high: the fair has handled over $400 million in sales. There is clearly a large market of people who want to own original, unique artworks but have what might be considered "normal" incomes. Most high-end art and antiquities are collected by a tiny minority of extremely wealthy individuals, institutions, and families, a sort of private club of just a few hundred millionaires the world over, many of whose families have been collecting art for centuries. This clubby atmosphere is cultivated by galleries and auction houses.

Having worked at Christie's, and knowing the art world from behind the scenes, I can attest to the widespread proactive encouragement of this sense of exclusivity. One of the reasons online art sales have never caught on for high-end objects is the social element of collecting: seeing and being seen, catching up with old friends, popping over to Milan for the Sotheby's sale, chatting about your latest purchase while poolside in Saint-Tropez, ostentatiously lending to the Met.

At the top level, art collecting has always been about two things: demonstrating one's erudition and showing off one's wealth. This dates back to Renaissance patrons, princes and popes, who sought top artists to decorate chapels and palaces which were designed to give the owner pleasure, sure, but just as much to awe his guests.

While you won't find Roman Abramovich or Bernard Arnault or Robbie Antonio (among Artnet's top ten collectors in the world) browsing the

Affordable Art Fair stalls, I wondered how the price of art affects desirability at all levels, and also how living artists price their works, striking the balance between a price someone might actually pay and a price high enough to make a potential buyer feel that the artist is serious and desired.

In my book on art forgery, I proposed an equation for the value of art: value = perceived (rarity + authenticity + demand). Most art is unique, so rarity refers to how many works by an artist exist at all (Giorgione died young and made far fewer paintings than his contemporary, Titian, so a Giorgione is far more valuable than a Titian). Authenticity is an issue for antiques and Old Masters, not usually a factor for the contemporary artists of the Affordable Art Fair. Demand, or the perception of it, is key to drive up the price. You need at least two people who really want to buy something, and the competition, particularly at auction, can make prices rise dramatically. The price for works by established artists is usually based on past sales—a Picasso with a similar provenance, importance, quality, and size that sold a few decades ago will be compared to a Picasso newly on the market and, after inflation, an estimated price is chosen. But the category of museum-quality art and antiques is its own rarified world, with a miniscule number of potential buyers functioning in a sociological bubble distinct from what might be called "normal folks."

What about contemporary artists who might show at the Affordable Art Fair? To find out how artists pick their prices, I spoke to several.

Painter Harry Hancock said, "Artists start by adding up materials and work hours—that becomes the base price, below which they are truly screwing themselves. But the intangible factors, such as virtuosity, originality, exclusivity, fame, talkability, can affect prices more dramatically." But not all these factors work for all artists. Hancock continues, "I base my works' value on what I consider the most solid pricing factors, like virtuosity and originality. . . . Virtuosity is extremely verifiable (it's pretty clear when it's not there) and enjoyable to look at." But fame is really the main driver. As Hancock says, "It holds a particular sway over art markets in our 'recommendation culture.'" Name recognition, either through the media or word of mouth within cadres of art collectors, surmounts all. There is a lot of art out there that does not display virtuosity that sells well, because some sort of buzz surrounds the artist. The million-dollar question, literally, is how to get that buzz, for with it comes fame, "talkability" (by which Hancock means a work of sufficient interest or shock value that it gets people talking), and the sense of exclusivity that prompts desire to own one of only a finite number of unique works by that artist.

Affordability is only really a factor for less-known artists, not established ones. Take Roman Uranjek, a famous artist, part of the IRWIN group, whose works feature in museum collections. He states, "My experience is that, in the art world, the name of the artist is a lot more important than the artwork itself. We live in the time of fetish, and the amount of sweat and tears put into the creation never represents the quality of the artworks, whereas the name of the artist does." Uranjek is renowned enough that he never prices his own work, because he, like all top artists, sells through a gallery or manager. But this must be earned. "The real value of the artwork comes with time, and with the artist's continuity."

Prices for people who are likely to buy at the Affordable Art Fair must be low enough to strike a balance between desire prompted almost exclusively by initial aesthetic appeal and a price point that feels doable. This sort of art is often wonderful, but it is usually a field of pleasant surprises. Buyers are unlikely to have heard of the artists showing there prior to seeing their work at the fair, and so the buzz is all but nonexistent. It is a starting point for artists who might hope to graduate into the "buzz zone" but are not yet there. Those not yet represented by galleries (which, by the way, regularly take 50 percent of the price for each work sold). This is a democratic, bricks-and-mortar pop-up art market, showcasing quality artists little to unknown to the cultured masses. Online galleries exist, trying to do something similar (like the new ArtOpen, which cleverly combines social media with art sales, as artists can upload their works, have them rated by other users, set a price, and receive 100 percent of what they ask for). Painter Nika Zupančič sees a problem in the availability of high-resolution digital imagery: "Nowadays there is no desire to possess something that you can virtually possess anytime." Those who might buy affordable art sometimes content themselves with a digital image or print, rather than the real thing. But there is a world of difference between seeing art in person, versus online. It is far easier to fall in love when admiring an object "in the flesh." Which is why an art fair will always trump an art website in encouraging sales.

I also spoke to two collectors about this issue, both of whom preferred to remain anonymous. One, who has an impressive collection of museum-quality works, valued in the low millions, said, "I think this is absolutely an issue, always has been, with the very best art by already famous artists, alive or long deceased. If I hear that a fellow collector (or a rival one) is interested, then my interest rises. We saw this as a proactive strategy with Saatchi. His enthusiasm for buying Young British Artists drew other collectors to them, afterward driving up the price of the works he'd already bought. It's like a run in the stock market. Then he sold high and moved on to young Chinese artists, with a similar effect." The other, who collects but with a normal-person, middle-class salary, particularly keen on mid-twentieth-century lithographs (you can get lithographs by the likes of Dalí, Chagall, and Miro for prices in the low thousands), said, "I'll want something when I see it, and then I always have to look at the price tag. The higher price will make me think more of the artist, that they must have admirers, but won't make me like the particular artwork more. It had me at hello, or it didn't have me at all. My interest in the price is not incentive to buy, but fear of not being able to afford. That's why the Affordable Art Fair is great for people like me, who like art but have to watch our pennies. I'll know that nothing there will be impossible for me to acquire, so I can relax and feel comfortable falling in love with any work I see there."

Art collecting must be divided into two halves for separate consideration. High price does encourage interest in the thin air of museum-quality sales and auctions. Back here on Earth, price gives the impression of an artist's growing fame, but it does not encourage purchases, largely for the reason of the limited wallet power of the potential buyer. In both worlds, price is equated with the (presumed) fame of the artist (a living artist can set very high prices and hope to impress), but in only one world does it encourage desire to own. For most, it's about the initial aesthetic and emotional impact, with the price tag as an afterthought. As Harry Hancock says, "The Affordable Art Fair is great because it provides a venue for art that shows virtuosity and originality, but no fame." It's fame, in the end, that pays.

Art Crime in Pop Culture: A Year in Review

It was in 2014 that art crime, particularly theft, seemed to crop up everywhere, and in surprising places. I was first taken by surprise when I realized, halfway through Wes Anderson's *Grand Budapest Hotel*, that there would be an art theft plot thrown into the mix. An Egon Schiele–like painting is snatched away from the eponymous hotel before it can be inherited by an undeserving relation. There is little more to it than that, the theft is merely a vehicle to add some plot to a film that is otherwise an excuse for a set-piece and its wonderfully weird inhabitants, but in the loosest sense of the word, it could qualify as an art heist film.

The next surprise came when I listened to the audiobook of Donna Tartt's Pulitzer Prize–winning novel, *The Goldfinch*. I knew that it was meant to be Dickensian, in its size, pace (following a single character from youth into adulthood, with microscopic detail that occasionally dragged the momentum to a near halt), and oddball characters, and that the plot surrounded a terrorist attack at the Metropolitan Museum of Art, and the titular painting, by the mysterious Carel Fabritius. But as the story wound on (and on and on—I felt compelled to finish it but never liked it particularly, most of all because I did not particularly like, nor care about, the protagonist, Theo Decker), I realized that Ms. Tartt had at least done her homework on the art crime side of things. She had clearly read up, almost certainly articles that my colleagues and I have written, because she paraphrases the lessons ARCA teaches about forgery, theft, and the illicit art market with admirable accuracy. A novice to the field can learn true facts about it through this work of fiction, so hats off. When a bomb explodes at the Met, killing Theo's mother, he finds himself carrying out of the museum a painting that a dying stranger urged him to take. His life unfolds, always with the hidden, lifted painting in the back of his mind, an anchor in his otherwise drifting, drug-addled, decidedly humorless existence (his lack of levity, fun, and humor is what prevented me from ever liking, and therefore cheering for, him). He becomes an antique furniture dealer, passes off some fakes, and then tries to recover *The Goldfinch*, rather against his will, when he realizes that a friend has stolen it from him. The details are well done, and I only wish that more authors (are you listening, Dan Brown) would follow the scrupulous research habits of Ms. Tartt. I only wish I liked the novel better.

The first compliment I will pay to the 2013 art heist movie, *The Art of the Steal*, is that it did not annoy me. That may sound like damning with faint praise, but I've got a good deal more praise to give, and this was its first major hurdle. There are benefits and burdens to possessing an expertise in a subject. I am a professor of art history specializing in the study of art crime—I write books on the subject, teach postgraduate courses, and lecture on the topic regularly. In short, I know too much to enjoy entertainments that get things wrong, or at least ostentatiously wrong. This does not. Jonathan Sobol's film is joyous, clever, and fun—everything an art heist movie should be.

Crunch Calhoun (Kurt Russell) and Nicky (Matt Dillon) play half-brothers who regularly stole art, their preferred scheme being to swap in a forgery for an original, often preferring to steal from criminals who already stole paintings, but know nothing about them, rather than trying to breach museums themselves. While swindling a Polish gangster out of a stolen Gauguin, Nicky got caught and offered up his brother Crunch to the police so he could get off. Crunch served five and a half years in a Polish prison, and is none too happy about it. When he gets out, he makes a meager living as a stunt motorcyclist, until he sees an opportunity, crystallized through the lens of being threatened by a goon who is actually after Nicky. Nicky invites him back into the game, and they plot a seemingly straightforward heist, recovering a rare book on behalf of its owner. They are pursued by an ingeniously comic Interpol agent and his assistant, a stone-faced Terence Stamp, a veteran art thief who is obliged to assist this investigation in order to get out of prison himself. Ticking all the boxes of the art heist genre, they assemble a team of crooks with special talents and punchy nicknames and set to work. But, as can be expected with such films, not all is as it seems, and there is a satisfying and surprising twist at the end that turns everything we thought (including some things that raised suspicions that the filmmaker was being sloppy) on its head.

Whether you consider this film to be an homage to the *Ocean's Eleven* series or a rip-off of it is really down to personal taste. It is safe to say that this film would not exist, certainly not in its present form, without the lucrative Clooney-Pitt-Damon franchise. On-screen graphics, the font on on-screen text, narrative voice-over, choice of lively music, split screen, colorful nicknames, heists, and double-crosses are all nicked straight from the three *Ocean's* movies. This style works well with the genre, a cross between caper and heist (capers being largely comical, heist films largely dramatic, but both about the mechanics and sleight of hand of the criminals). But the tone is fun, the film genuinely funny at times, and the plotline sufficiently well researched so as to raise no hackles on this audience member, who is notoriously annoyed when film, fiction, and the media get things wrong, as they so often do, about art crime.

In putting *The Art of the Steal* to the test, let us consider what it gets wrong about real art thefts, but also praise what it gets right. Writer-director Jonathan Sobol clearly did his homework, and what it gets wrong it appears to choose to get wrong, for the sake of the plot and in the name of artistic license, while what it gets right shows an intelligence and research behind a light entertainment that this occasionally curmudgeonly professor appreciates.

Ten Things It Got Wrong (But Forgivably So)

1. There is no such thing as an Interpol agent, in the sense of a detective out in the field, investigating and chasing bad guys. Interpol is an administrative body that coordinates data from world police departments. Police do the investigating, Interpol files their reports. So to have an "Interpol agent" as adversary of our band of crooks is like having an air traffic controller who is also flying a plane. Police, likewise, do not work alone, especially not with a convicted criminal in tow. It is true that most major stolen art recoveries are thanks to information gleaned from paid criminal informants who are on police payrolls, but these informants do reveal themselves and do not accompany police on their investigations, as Terence Stamp's dour convict does here.
2. There is likewise, with very few exceptions throughout the history of art crime, no such thing as a professional art thief. There have been some criminals who have stolen art more than once, but the idea that there are career specialists who earn their illicit living by stealing art is largely fictitious. There are career art forgers and *tombaroli*, tomb raiders, who

are professional robbers of antiquities buried in the earth, but not so for thieves of art from museums and private collections.

3. The opening heist, in Poland, is very kind to Polish museum practices—kinder than fact. A character comments that all of the paintings in a Polish museum are alarmed. When last I heard, there was actually only one artwork in all of Poland's rich museum that had its own, individual alarm system (as opposed to a general security system for the museum itself)—Leonardo's *Lady with an Ermine*. It is generous of the filmmaker to credit a random Warsaw museum with elaborate security measures for every one of its paintings.
4. When Nicky is arrested, he is threatened with twenty years in prison. Art thieves get off far lighter than that, with sentences of two to four years far more common. The longest sentence ever given out to someone involved in stolen and looted art was the ten-year sentence Giacomo Medici received for trafficking in hundreds of looted antiquities—and he was no small-time thief, but the head of an elaborate criminal ring with its tentacles in many nations, selling looted works to world-renowned museums.
5. The opening heist is predicated on the fact that a Polish gangster would bother bringing a freshly stolen Gauguin to a museum conservation department to be authenticated. Criminals involved in art almost never know anything about art, nor have any interest in it, but they likewise would not bother to get a work authenticated. The moment a theft hits the news, the media does the authenticating on the criminal's behalf, publishing a detailed description of exactly what was stolen and how valuable it is.
6. Most criminals know nothing about art. There is a running joke that all but one of the characters mispronounce the name of the French pointillist painter Georges Seurat. There is likewise confusion (intentionally sown, it turns out) over a book supposedly printed by Gutenberg. The band of thieves tell the story of Valfierno and the theft of the *Mona Lisa* as if it is real, which bothered me until it was revealed as a plot device. A 1932 article in the *Saturday Evening Post* by Karl Decker purported to convey the story of an Argentine count, Valfierno, who hired Vincenzo Peruggia to steal the *Mona Lisa* not to own it himself or sell the original, but to trick six dumb American millionaires into buying forgeries of the *Mona Lisa*, each thinking that they secretly had purchased the stolen original. That entire story was fabricated, but it infected the popular imagination and perpetuated many myths about art theft, including . . .
7. The myth of the stolen art collector. The film includes characters who regularly buy stolen art and have secret collections of it. This is another common misconception, perpetuated by fiction, film, and sloppy journalism.

In reality we know of only around two dozen "criminal art collectors" in history—a negligible number, when you consider that there are tens of thousands of art thefts reported every year.

8. It is a fun idea to pair forgers with thieves, but this does not happen in real life. Art forgers tend to work alone or in pairs (with a con man) and are rarely involved in organized crime. Art theft is largely the realm of organized crime, from small local gangs (like Calhoun's) to large international syndicates. The closest that forgery comes to involvement in art theft took place in Poland—thieves swapped a framed poster of a Monet, bought at the gift shop, for the real thing, which they lifted from the museum's wall. So much for well-alarmed Polish collections.
9. The characters use the terms "fake" and "forgery" interchangeably, but they are actually two different things. A fake is an original object that is altered in some way to increase its value in a fraudulent manner. A forgery is a whole new object, made from scratch, in fraudulent imitation of something more valuable. But that is truly splitting hairs—which I only do because the film got so much right.
10. The criminals in this gang are more worldly, witty, and clever than their real-life counterparts. This is fair enough, because it is more fun to watch a movie featuring smart, interesting protagonists. They show a great sense of humor in their choice of modern sculpture in which to hide a forged Gutenberg book (it is a giant, cubic replica of the female anatomy). Our gang has watched their share of art heist movies and suggest schemes borrowed from them: a "Trojan horse" object, as seen in *The Thomas Crown Affair*, and "cat suits," as seen in *Entrapment*, for instance.

The Art of the Steal is great fun, and unlike in most films of this sort, knowing more about the subject offers some rewards, rather than limiting its entertainment value because of mistakes it might make. An art expert in the film has the surname Panofsky, a reference to Irwin Panofsky, one of the greatest twentieth-century art historians. And it gets a lot right. An enraged gangster who threatens Crunch demands either a stolen Seurat that Nicky lifted off him or $30,000. That sounds about right—stolen art seems to have a value of around 7 to 10 percent of its legitimate auction value, a fact we know because that is the amount that desperate criminals have asked undercover cops to pay them for stolen art. The asking price, $30,000, might just be around 7 percent of the legitimate value of a small Seurat. Hats off to Jonathan Sobol and his team of art thieves. They got a surprising amount of detail correct, and that which they got wrong was either volitional or meant to facilitate plot, and forgivable in the context of artistic license. Why they chose to give their film the same title as a critically acclaimed documentary is another question, but perhaps in this case, stealing titles is as apt as paintings.

Banksy's Shredder Is More Ingenious than You Realize

Whether you consider his recent headline-grabber to be a great work of performance art in absentia, a prank sticking a middle finger up at the art world, a brilliant piece of publicity, or all of the above, there is no denying that Banksy is having the most fun of any artist, perhaps in history. We have examined his identity, almost certainly one half of the famous musical act Massive Attack, in a past column and he is known for his graffiti art, his tongue-in-cheek sleights of hand (consider his documentary entitled *Exit through the Gift Shop*), and his recent large-scale installation, Dismaland, a functional, horrifying worst amusement park ever conceptual work that is unique in its scale and interactive three-dimensional satire. His latest is a doozy, but it is also a completely brilliant way to quickly and artificially inflate the value of his own art, though any psychologist studying him would be quick to say that he is in it not for the money but for the laughs.

For anyone who missed it, at a recent Sotheby's auction, a spray-painting by Banksy, entitled *Girl with Balloon*, was sold for a record-tying one million pounds. As soon as the hammer fell, an alarm sounded within the gilded frame of the painting and it began to shred, dropping slowly down through a shredder that was hidden within the frame of the print that was displayed on the wall in the auction room. The newly purchased £1 million painting was thus sliced into dozens of vertical strips as it floated to the ground.

The first thought was that this destroyed an object that had just been purchased for seven figures. What had the buyer acquired and would he be forced to pay for it? It was designed to self-destruct and it was, of course, the artist who arranged it (he sent the first Instagram of it happening). Was he making fun of the market for his own work? On the one hand yes, but on the other hand, he was doing the buyer a great favor. Works of art that are the subject of controversy, especially those stolen or attacked, see a sharp rise in value, thanks to the notoriety and media emerging from such misadventures. People who otherwise have no interest in art in general, or this artist in particular, will suddenly know all about it, thereby attracting the interest of potential buyers who might not otherwise have entered the fray, and highlighting this particular work as of enough interest to spark the attention of criminals or evildoers and, subsequently, the media. Historically, there is a direct correlation between media reports about the high values for which art sells at auction and criminals trying to target those very same works or works by the same artist. Media fuels both criminal and popular interest.

Banksy knows this very well, and so it is no surprise that various art trade talking heads, when interviewed after this event, said that the shredding of the work made its value at least double. But Banksy was doing something that has not been discussed yet, and that is transforming a spray-painting, which Banksy makes by simply spraying through a stencil, and for which there are multiple versions of any one painting (making it effectively more like a print than a one-off painting in the traditional sense), into a unique work.

By definition, works that appear as multiples in a series are of less value than unique works, because they are less rare—there are X number of them, instead of just one. This makes them more affordable, which can spread notoriety, as was the case with Albrecht Dürer who, during the Renaissance, focused on printmaking, trademarking his monogram signature, and used the portability and affordability of prints to become Europe's most famous artist, at a time when Raphael and Leonardo and Titian and Michelangelo were vying for that title. Banksy's popularity for the general public is down to his witty graffiti art and the game with his identity, but he is the darling of mid-level collectors precisely because of his affordability. People of moderate wealth who wish to buy into trendy art can afford a Banksy (his paintings, like this one, are usually sold in the mid six figures, and his prints sell for the low five figures, which is a very reasonable amount of money, in high-end art terms). And so making prints and multiple spray-paintings allow for a democratization and enhanced quantity of potential collectors.

But Banksy did something brilliant with his shredder gag. He transformed a spray-painting, which is so easily and inexpensively produced with a simple stencil and a can of spray paint, essentially costing him nothing in terms of time and raw material, into a unique work. He did so through a work of performance art. He was in the audience at the auction house, designed the action, and so while he did not make his presence known to those in the room, he was the actor in his own dramatic moment. Performance art is only enjoyed by those physically there to see it. But it can leave traces, like photographs and videos and written or spoken accounts by eyewitnesses. It can also leave relics that collectors love to snap up. In this case, the "relic," the painting in question, was purchased seconds before the performance began. Thus the value of the work is increased in three distinct ways: What was once just one of a series of spray-paintings became a unique work, the only one in shreds. The spray-painting also became the primary relic of a singular performance. And it was effectively "attacked," though the attack was planned and carried out by the artist himself, making it the target of the sort of (usually criminal) activity that the media loves to report on.

Presumably, the owner of this newly shredded, newly purchased painting took possession of the shredder frame and the dozens of long vertical slices that now represent the carcass of the work and will reassemble them into a unique work by one of the hottest artists in the world. Its resale value, prestige, and cachet are now tremendous and far greater than the painting alone. It seems probable that Sotheby's was in on the gag, seeing as this was the last lot in the auction (it would have disturbed proceedings unpleasantly had it not been the last lot sold), and I'd say good for them for having a sense of humor (which is too often lacking in the art trade).

What appeared at first to be a tongue-in-cheek mocking prank, and then which also appeared to be a very clever publicity stunt, and then appeared to be a disaster for the buyer, is actually a clever way to immediately transform a painting that probably cost less than twenty pounds to produce and a few hundred to frame, and which sold for one million pounds and is now worth many times that, thanks to a most singular destructive intervention.

How Not to Buy Stolen, Looted, or Forged Art

No one wants to be the subject of a big "oops." The Del Sole family bought an $8.3 million Rothko painting from the Knoedler Gallery that turned out to be by some Chinese guy they'd never heard of. Oops. Steven Spielberg bought a $200,000 Norman Rockwell that turned out to have been stolen from a St. Louis gallery. Oops. And if you buy an antiquity these days that emerged from Syria, your purchase might be funding fundamentalist terrorists. Big oops.

In order to avoid aforementioned oopses, art collectors need to be informed. But the art trade has long thrived on the fact that so-called experts know much more about the works in question than the buyers. The high-end art market is, and always has been, one of the least-transparent multibillion-dollar markets in the world. Can you imagine buying, say, a very expensive house for $1 million when you don't know the current owner or how they acquired it, there is little or no paperwork attesting to its ownership history and upkeep, its price feels fairly arbitrary. And even though it looks like it's made of bricks, you can't really be certain, they insist on cash (possibly wired to a Swiss bank account), and you're not permitted to investigate further before purchasing. Sound good? Welcome to the art world, where this sort of thing is normal, and has been for centuries. The opacity of the art trade has several facets. When the first auction houses, Sotheby's and Christie's, were first established, in the eighteenth century, their main business was liquidating the art collections of once-wealthy aristocrats who could no longer afford a life of luxury, what with the Industrial Revolution changing the way money was earned and the feudal system out the window. Those aristocrats didn't want to advertise their financial straits, and the auctioneers obliged by refusing to divulge the seller, simply referring to them as a "lady" or a "gentleman." Even today, police sometimes need a warrant to oblige galleries or auction houses to reveal who consigned works to them. Then there's the knowledge gap. Although it probably should be, there's never been a tradition of buyers insisting on seeing forensic test results indicating the authenticity of a work that is for sale. Buyers are told about the work by the expert—as much as the expert is willing to reveal about its authorship, subject matter, state of conservation, background story, provenance—and that's it. Take it or leave it. If I were dropping a million on a painting (or a house, for that matter), I would not buy anything without knowing the owner, and without independent test results that indicated that the work is what the expert is telling me it is. But then again, I'm a professor specializing in the study of art crime (and I don't sell enough books to drop a million on anything).

As the author of several books on art crime, and having taught the history of art crime for many years, I know scores of tricks that thieves, forgers, and con men have used successfully in the past. We study history so as not to repeat past mistakes, and from these case studies, we can draw lessons on how not to be fooled in the future. Clever con men will always find new ways to deceive, and it is much more likely that an expert will err without malicious intent, rather than proactively try to commit fraud, but forewarned is forearmed. With the Frieze Art Fair fast approaching, it's a good time to look at five tips for how to buy legal, authentic art, wherever you may be, whatever style you prefer, and whatever your budget.

Check with a Stolen Art Database . . . but That's Only the Start

In order not to be criminally liable should you (inadvertently) purchase stolen art, you need to be able to demonstrate two things: due diligence and a good faith purchase. Good faith means that you must be able to argue that you genuinely thought the object was legitimate when you purchased it. Due diligence means that you checked around, for example, with stolen art databases (like the one run by the Art Recovery Group), and the object wasn't listed. This is a bare minimum, but just because a work is not listed as having been stolen doesn't mean it's not problematic (for example, any antiquity looted directly from the earth will not appear, because it was last seen centuries or millennia ago).

Ask about the Provenance, Then Actively Check It

Provenance is the documented history of an object. If you can't trace the entire history of an object, that is not in itself cause for suspicion—few objects, aside from the very recent, have a complete ownership history. But ask about provenance. Antiquities must be accompanied by documentation that proves they were excavated and exported prior to 1970 in order to be tradeable (prior to the UNESCO Convention that year, laws were disjointed and irregularly enforced, so a sort of amnesty is given to objects traded before that date). The more provenance there is, the safer you can feel that the work is a) authentic, if it has a charted history of people thinking it was authentic, and b) not stolen or looted. But few people check the provenance itself. If, say, a painting purports to have been exhibited at three different galleries, each of the galleries and exhibition dates should be checked. Red flags are raised when none of the provenance can be easily double-checked (if all three galleries are now closed, or the past owners are all deceased). Sometimes crooks indicate provenance that is not actually related to the object in question.

Look at the Back of Works, Outside of Their Frames

Backs of paintings and prints (and bottoms of sculptures) contain a wealth of information: things like stickers or stamps from past owners or sellers, customs permissions, as well as the normal wear and tear that you'd expect from an object that may be hundreds of years old. Forgers tend to be lazy about doctoring the parts of the works that are normally hidden. The most frequently forged type of art is the twentieth-century lithograph print, by the likes of Dalí, Miro, Chagall, and Picasso (who is also, by far, the most frequently forged artist). These are normally sold nicely matted and framed, and it seems a shame to dismantle them to look at the back of the work. But a quality laser print on fancy paper made last Tuesday looks almost exactly like a lithograph from the 1950s when encased in glass, so collectors should feel empowered to insist that they see all sides of the art they're planning to buy.

Ask about Forensic Testing

There's no good reason why forensic testing of artworks prior to sale is not standard. Buyers don't insist, so there's no incentive for sellers to do it—we're supposed to rely exclusively on expert opinion. But I always advise collectors to inquire about forensic test results, and if there are none, to ask if you could pay for forensic testing yourself, prior to purchase. Testing these days is not necessarily invasive and might cost as little as a few hundred bucks. Not much for peace of mind when you're about to pay six or seven figures. Then gauge the reaction of the seller. If they refuse, consider walking away. I wouldn't buy a used car unless my mechanic checks it first . . .

Do Not Buy Any Antiquity That May Have Come from Conflict Zones, Like Syria and Iraq

Recent documentaries and investigations have shown how some bad seeds in the art trade knowingly sell antiquities looted or stolen from conflict zones, which can mean that your purchase is funding terrorists (if you want to see how this works, check out the film *Blood Antiques*). Don't be a party to this, even unwittingly. It's hard to request a moratorium on buying antiquities from the Levant, but unless they come with extensive (and verifiable) provenance to show they've been in foreign collections for decades, I wouldn't even consider them.

Learning from the Museum of the Bible: Five Tips on How Not to Buy Looted Antiquities

It is tempting to feel that some cosmic justice has been meted out to the Museum of the Bible, which recently admitted that five items in its collection that it believed were authentic Dead Sea Scrolls have been tested and are now considered to be forgeries. This came after the decision, in 2017, that the museum's owners, the Green family of Hobby Lobby store fame (as well as religious fundamentalist fame, having successfully sued the US government because it did not want taxes from its employee health plans to go to contraceptives), had purchased looted antiquities, and were forced to pay a fine and return some 5,500 illicit objects that had been bought by dealers in Israel and the United Arab Emirates in 2010. Neither of these revelations come as a surprise to those who know how the collection of the Museum of the Bible was amassed. Most of the objects were bought en masse from other collections without knowing (or caring to look too closely) at how they were initially acquired. The Greens' collection and how it was gathered have raised no shortage of eyebrows, and so a bit of schadenfreude can be expected. But kudos to the Museum of the Bible for not trying to cover up the latest scandal, but admitting it, with however much chagrin.

With this in mind, the reasonable question may rise as to how collections and individuals can avoid these sorts of problems. We have already delved into how to avoid accidentally buying fakes and forgeries in this essay, but what about not accidentally (or on purpose) buying looted antiquities?

Here are five tips to take with you on your next trip to an art fair, gallery, auction, or even flea markets on some back streets.

1. The first thing that you need to know is that, until 1970, the laws about buying cultural heritage objects and exporting them were quite chaotic and irregularly enforced and differed from nation to nation. That is why the 1970 UNESCO Convention is so important: it essentially codified and formalized and made more complicated bureaucratically the ways cultural heritage objects could be excavated and exported for sale abroad. So, any object that was excavated and exported after 1970 should have a good deal of paperwork accompanying it to ensure its legality. But the convention also granted an informal amnesty for objects excavated and exported prior to 1970. For this reason, you may encounter doctored paperwork suggesting that an object up for sale was exported prior to 1970, which can be used to excuse its lack of proper paperwork. This may be true, but it also is a trick that troublemakers use to make a newly excavated antiquity appear legal.
2. In the world of fine art, the more provenance, the documented history of an object, that can be found, the better. But in the world of antiquities, sometimes there is little to no paper trail. That doesn't necessarily mean that the object was looted, but any antiquity that has been outside of its find country long enough ago should have some sort of trail of paperwork that suggests that it had a long enough biography to match its alleged excavation and exportation dates. So be very suspicious of antiquities that have no accompanying documentation, or very little, and especially be ready to walk away if any dealer refuses to talk about the origin of objects or to provide you with any paperwork. That is an immediate red flag.
3. Then comes the second step. There is such a focus on provenance that sometimes people look for quantity without looking at the content. Whenever presented with documentation reported to be associated with a certain object, you must be very careful to make sure that a) the provenance documents are not forgeries, and b) that even if the paperwork is authentic, that it does truly refer to the object in question. Appropriating one document and trying to pass it off as referring to an object that was recently looted is a not-uncommon trick of the trade. So, don't look just for quantity of documentation but look very hard at the documentation itself.
4. In order not to get into trouble for having accidentally purchased a looted antiquity, a buyer must be able to prove two things in court. One is "due

diligence," which means that you can show that you made a reasonable effort to ensure that the object in question does not appear on any stolen art database or police record of stolen or looted objects. This is basically demonstrating that did your homework to make sure that there was no obvious notice that the object in question is problematic. The second component is that you have to be a "good faith" purchaser. That means that you have to be able to demonstrate that you genuinely thought the object was legit when you purchased it. This second component is rather nebulous, and one could see how it would be fairly easy for an unscrupulous type to take advantage of these two proofs. Unless someone wrote a diary entry that reads, "Dear diary, I just bought an antiquity that I know was looted but bought it anyway," then it is quite easy to prove good faith. We mentioned that due diligence involves checking stolen art databases and police lists of stolen art. But what sometimes happens is that a buyer will check an antiquity against such a database, knowing it will not appear there, because such databases only contain objects that were reported as having been stolen from extant collections, and therefore they could never list antiquities taken directly from clandestine archeological excavations. Aware of this, a buyer or dealer could prove due diligence by checking such a database, receiving a document attesting to the fact that it did not appear in the database, and therefore protect themselves with the excuse that they didn't know that the object in question was looted. It is a bit too easy to pretend that you didn't know, and even to have documents supporting this argument, when you probably did. The laws currently in place are beneficial to troublemakers.

5. The vast majority of the art trade is 100 percent well-meaning and acts legally. There is a very tiny handful of bad guys who work within it and take advantage of the odd and murky organism that is the art trade. But there is a good deal of what I tend to call "non-malevolent wishful thinking." That is to say that almost no one is doing anything that they would identify as illegal, but there is a large measure of subconscious wishing that any new antiquity that comes on the market would be authentic and legitimate. If it is, many people benefit. The seller makes money, the middlemen make their commission, scholars have a new object to study, and the buyer has a new trophy. So, there's a marginal propensity to hope that every object is legit, and then to perhaps overlook questionable aspects of it because of that enthusiasm. This is really what buyers have to be wary of, from private individuals looking for souvenirs to giant, multimillion-dollar museums.

Is *I Love Dick*'s Hunky Art-Throb Actually a Good Artist?

Living in the wilds of central Europe, I'm often late—often several years late—for trending US entertainment. I watched *Arrested Development*, season 1, for the first time in 2013. So, I'm feeling rather edgy that I recently binge-watched *I Love Dick*, having grown intrigued by reading an interview with the male lead, Kevin Bacon, in *Esquire*. While I enjoyed the show's trainwreck-y drive, I was struck by the artwork created by Bacon's character, an art instructor and internationally renowned Texan artist/cowboy, whom the creators named Dick Jarrett. It's a reasonable question to ask whether Dick's art is any good. But the real question is whether what the creators envisioned their character might create is any good, good enough to make feasible his fictional status as a world-famous sculptor and land artist.

Most viewers will recall a key sculpture in the series that is accidentally bumped off its plinth and broken: the work is, unsurprisingly, called *Untitled* and consists of exactly one found object, a brick. "I like a straight line," Dick explains, defending his work after he just slammed the pretentious, boring art film made by Chris Kraus, the woman who becomes obsessed with him. In a later episode, this same brick will be rearranged into a stack of its broken parts, creating something we are meant to see as significantly better than the found object alone.

The creators, including *Transparent* genius Jill Soloway, wound up borrowing ideas from existing artists to create their Dick's creations. That's fair enough, and I'd wager that 98 percent of the show's viewers would not recognize the sources of inspiration for the art included. But for the 2 percent of us that do, it's a fun game to play. And I'll be honest—if Dick Jarrett were a real artist, I'd be a fan.

Consider the brick. The history of using found objects as art, also called "ready-mades," links back most prominently to the sculptures "by" Marcel Duchamp, including his seminal (or should it be "urinal") *Fountain* of 1917, a century ago, when he purchased a urinal, turned it on its side, signed the name of an invented artist upon it ("R. Mutt," which was inspired by the urinal company), and proclaimed it one of the greatest sculptures of its time (he also did not officially claim to have been the artist behind it, though he was fooling no one). The most famous recent example is Tracey Emin's *My Bed*, in which she preserved her own bed after a multiweek binge of self-destructive behavior (sex, drugs, smoking, alcohol . . . one presumes some rock 'n' roll) and considered it a snapshot of herself at the time. It sold for over a million and attracts hundreds of thousands of admirers every year to see it on display.

But bricks, as objects, have also been featured in art. My own publisher, Phaidon, has an illustrated book entitled *Brick*, which features many a photo of . . . well, you guessed it. But the most infamous ready-made brick sculpture is *Equivalent* by Carl Andre, which my *Guardian* colleague, art critic Jonathan Jones, tore apart, and which I will agree is more interesting to think about than to look at. It consists of purchased bricks laid in an orderly stack. That's it. Dick's brick is just a solitary individual perched upon a plinth. If you like it, it's about the artist seeing art in something "ordinary." If you don't like it, then you can certainly say, "It's just a brick." I sympathize with this knee-jerk response. But as a riposte, I would quote my friend, the great conceptual artist Ulay, who has said about conceptual art, "Some can't, others don't."

In terms of Dick's uber-macho, cowboy personality, there are any number of potential real artists to call upon. There is also Dick Hebdige, the real-life cultural theorist upon whom Dick is based (the author of the novel *I Love Dick*, which inspired the series, has stated that Hebdige was the inspiration but tried to change as much as possible about the character so as not to incur his wrath, though he nevertheless filed a cease-and-desist order against her and is no fan of either the book or the series). Richard Serra, Donald Judd, Richard Long, Jeff Koons, Damien Hirst are all known for a measure of machismo.

Dick's closest comparison in the art world is Donald Judd, a pioneer of ready-mades. While born in Missouri, his foundation is based in Marfa, Texas, where all the action in *I Love Dick* takes place, and Judd is the reason why Marfa actually is, in real life, a destination for artists and writers. Judd's Chinati Foundation, in Marfa, has a permanent collection featuring works by the likes of, you guessed it, Carl Andre and Richard Long, as part of a 340-acre desert plot of land.

In the 1960s, Judd proactively turned against what he considered traditional, European art values and focused on "specific objects," which included ready-mades, purchased and arranged by the artist but not "made" by him. He also combined sculpture with architecture and land art, blurring the boundaries, as in his 1977 *Untitled* (calling your work *Untitled* represents a thoroughly unhelpful shrug of the shoulders, but it has been the hip thing to do since the sixties), which consists of Corten steel rings in an outdoor landscape in Munster, Germany. He preferred "plain and simple" art, focusing on angles and sheets and clean lines. He's the sort of artist who would certainly have said, "I like a straight line." He famously floated a basketball in a glass tank of water.

But the most striking art shown in the show as having been made by Dick Jarrett appears to have been inspired by Richard Long. The British artist is known for works like *Houghton Cross*, an X made of slate stones; *Full Moon Circle*, a circle of flat stones that looks like a reflecting pool; and *A Line in Norfolk* which, as the title suggests, is a razor-straight line of ochre-colored found stones. There is a canal gouged arrow-straight into the earth, running as far into the distance as the eye can see. There is a usable sculpture in the form of Dick's swimming pool, a perfectly round concrete saucer floating above the vast, wild desert expanse (into which Dick plunges naked at the end of the first episode, and into which Chris Kraus dips near the end of the series). But most memorable is the climactic work that Dick makes before "quitting" art and leaving Marfa. Inspired by a sidewinder snake, he creates a writhe of boulders in a form that art historians would call *figura serpentinata*, a snake-like S shape, which Michelangelo described as the most beautiful pose into which your subject might be contorted (he established mannerism, which featured unrealistically contorted figures, bent for dramatic effect). It is beautiful and interesting and distinctive and the sort of thing we art historians can write much about. Is it ready-made art? It is, in the sense that Richard Long makes ready-mades, often out of found natural, rather than man-made objects.

If the invented Dick Jarrett and the works he is meant to have made indeed qualify as great art, then does that make Jill Soloway and her collaborators, those who conceived of Dick's art, themselves great artists? Yes, if you consider making quality television an art form. But they are more paying homage to a mosaic of established, real-life artists, riffing on the work of others to create Dick's oeuvre. But there's an art to that, as well. After all, perhaps the art of others can be considered as found objects, ready-mades that a third party can appropriate, reinstall in a slightly different way, and then call their own.

The Lost Art of Art Exhibitions?

We're experiencing an extended period during which actual art exhibits in brick-and-mortar museums cannot be visited. The pandemic and periodic lockdowns to combat it mean that it's ill-advised to linger among crowds of strangers in closed spaces, which counts out enjoying art in public. Some might consider this a death knell for traditional museums and galleries. From the perspective of income from visitors, it is certainly catastrophic. But my feeling and hope is that an alternative, parallel type of art-going experience will emerge from all this and remain when normalcy returns. As standard practice, I would love to see virtual exhibits run in parallel to brick-and-mortar shows.

Just before the pandemic, February 2020, I was fortunate enough to take one last trip. I was invited to speak at a conference in Ghent, Belgium, organized by the police to discuss the newly opened blockbuster *Van Eyck: An Optical Revolution* exhibit there. We speakers got the chance to privately view the magnificent exhibit which brought together, for the first time and probably the last, nearly every painting by Jan van Eyck, including the newly restored *Ghent Altarpiece* (the subject of one of my books, hence my involvement). The exhibit was a huge success, sold out for months and with plans to extend it. But then, a few weeks later, the pandemic reared its head fully and disaster struck for the world and, of course, for in-person visits to exhibits.

Back home in isolation, I found myself taking virtual tours of sites of cultural and historical interest with my five- and seven-year-old daughters. There is no large trove of these virtual tours in one spot. We had to seek them out. Sometimes we found on YouTube simple walk-throughs filmed and posted by visitors with decent cameras. Other times we were grateful to find official walk-through videos made by the institutions, or even virtual reality or augmented reality systems in which, video game style, we could control our pace moving through a space and choose what we looked at, with occasional didactic material popping up, as in the virtual tour of the Tomb of Pharaoh Ramses VI. I found myself wishing that there were more of these virtual tours, of better quality, with more optional information if we sought a deeper experience. This is rarely done, but I'm grateful when it is.

As if in answer to my wishes, the Van Eyck exhibit later released just this: a 360-degree virtual tour featuring 120 artworks and divided in two: a version for adults and a version specifically for kids. They kindly make it available for free, but I would not mind making a small donation for the privilege of engaging in such wonderful exhibits from afar. I live in Slovenia and, with young children, travel as little as possible. This means that I miss 99 percent of the art exhibits that I'd love to see, not to mention the permanent exhibits that are in places I've not yet, or may never, visit in person. Making such virtual tours a standard accompaniment to both permanent collections and temporary exhibits would vastly increase the exposure of the host institutions and their exhibits. This has been done in the realm of concerts and sporting events. Let it become standard for art shows, too.

One might argue that access to virtual tours will result in fewer people attending art shows in person. If you've been to The Venetian in Las Vegas, who needs to fly to Venice, right? It doesn't work that way. As Adam Gopnik recently argued in an article about the Louvre, the endless run of selfies, merchandise, and images of Leonardo's *Mona Lisa* have whetted appetites to see the painting in person, not acted as a stand-in for visiting it. A virtual tour doesn't check off a box on a bucket list. My Instagram feed is mostly crowded with photos of burgers, but I still want to eat them. Interest piqued virtually, through video and photo, stimulates understanding and interest in what we see. If and when we can, we still want to see them in person. The experience of art "in the flesh" is a whole level up from anything virtual—it is a sensory experience, deep and visceral. But engaging with art virtually is far preferable to not being able to engage at all.

Then there are exhibits made exclusively for virtual enjoyment. I just curated one such exhibit, in collaboration with ARCA and Samsung. *Missing Masterpieces* features twelve high-resolution images of lost paintings, by the likes of Van Gogh and Monet, objects that we could not visit in person even if we wished to because they were stolen, mislaid, possibly buried with their owner, even likely destroyed. The exhibit is available to anyone online for free, as well as to anyone with a Samsung Frame TV. There is virtual wall copy for each painting, telling its story, and an interactive component—almost all of these works are out there somewhere and viewers are encouraged to write in with ideas about where they might be or tips that might lead to their recovery. This sort of "impossible exhibit" can only exist in the virtual sphere and so it perfectly embraces the concept of virtual exhibits.

As I write this (this was written during the pandemic), virtual tours are still all we can enjoy. Perhaps the silver lining will be making standard a virtual accompaniment to the world's collections and great exhibits, democratizing who can see the art and learn from it. Inspired by this, just as many people, if not more, will travel to see the exhibits in person. But the art can be enjoyed by all, even if the experience won't be as deep and primal.

Yet virtual experiences can advance scholarship where in-person visits cannot. I wrote my book on *The Ghent Altarpiece* and spent countless hours with it, in person or examining photos of it in books. Yet I never noticed a particular figure within the painting, laughing maniacally, nor did I read about him in any of the previous books on what is arguably the most important painting ever made, until I was able to examine a billion-pixel version of it. This allowed me to zoom in with such detail and clarity that I was able to spot this figure I'd never been able to see in person. A virtual experience of high quality is not just second prize to being there in person but may offer fresh revelations.

4 THEFT AND SECURITY

Dürer's Rhinoceros: On Nazi Book Theft

Until the late 1930s, German children taught about rhinoceroses would have flipped their textbooks not to a photograph, but to a 1515 woodcut print by an artist who had never actually seen such a creature in the flesh. The artist, Albrecht Dürer, was the greatest in Germanic history, and the print is spectacular. It happens to be a pretty good impression of a rhino, but not one by an eyewitness. A real rhino had been on display in Lisbon in 1515, brought there in 1513 from India. Dürer was sent a description and a sketch of that rhino by another artist, and from this he prepared his woodcut. But while it is a wonderful artwork, it is not accurate and certainly not scientific. Dürer shows the animal covered in bony plates, as if it is wearing a natural suit of armor, complete with a throat protector (gorget) and what look like rivets linking together various "plates." It is rhino-as-medieval-knight. He also shows the rhino as scaled, like a lizard (though some scholars argue that this is a representation of the dermatitis from which the captive rhino suffered after its four-month sea voyage from India to Portugal). Enthusiasm for Dürer overrode the desire for scientific accuracy. Even when photographs of rhinos were available, even when you could see a real rhino at the zoo and recognize the inaccuracy of Dürer's version, the print remained the exemplar of rhinocerosness in reference books for schoolchildren.

Which brings me to Nazi book theft.

The scale of book theft during the Second World War is immense, far dwarfing the already boggling numbers of Nazi art theft. While some have estimated that five million art objects changed hands inappropriately during the Second World War, most of them stolen or appropriated by the Nazis, few have discussed the Nazi practice of looting books, rare and otherwise, from the libraries of conquered Europe. *The Book Thieves*, a book by Swedish journalist Anders Rydell, focuses on just this. Beyond the book burnings, book theft was engaged on an unimaginable scale. In an interview with the *European Review*, Rydell explains that it "dwarfed the art looting," with an estimated one to two hundred million books stolen during the war.

While it feels more logical to steal art (some of which was exhibited as "degenerate," some of which was sold to foreign collectors—including American and British—to finance the Nazi war effort, some of which was kept by avaricious Nazi higher-ups for their personal delectation, some of which was intended for Hitler's planned "super museum" at Linz), since it has an obvious value, financially in terms of sale, symbolically in terms of capturing the treasures of the vanquished, and aesthetically, books are a rather different proposition. Sure, rare books and manuscripts can have a sale value rivaling artworks, but most of the books stolen by the Nazis were not financially valuable. The Nazi art theft bureau, the ERR (Einsatzstab Reichsleiter Rosenberg), was originally founded to seize documents and archives that had a strategic value to the Third Reich and only later began to consume artworks, too. And therein lies a clue.

Rydell's analysis of why the Nazis took so many books reveals some chilling rationales. "The looting had mainly two purposes," he said. "On the one hand, to 'unarm' their enemies by taking the weapons of thought—books, libraries, archives. In Poland, the Nazis even looted books from schools—in a Nazi-dominated East, Polish children didn't have any need for higher education as, in the future, they would be reduced to slaves under the master race." Kafka once said, "A book must be an axe for the frozen sea within us." The Nazis aimed to disarm those they wished to see subdued by removing the weapons of thought.

Rydell continues, explaining that "the second goal was even more devious. By looting the libraries and archives of their enemies, the Nazis tried to take control over the memory and history of the victims. Alfred Rosenberg, who founded the Institute for the Study of the Jewish Question (and, not coincidentally, the ERR, which even bears his name), was afraid that, even if the Nazis won the war, future generations would judge them for their crimes. Therefore, it was important to control the memory of Jews, not as a way to eradicate them from written memory, but to establish the Jews as an incarnation of evil for all future generations." Thus it was not for profit, but for posterity, and the ability to control it. The Nazis sought to wipe Europe's libraries clean and to rewrite a version of history that best suited their spin.

This is where the example of Dürer's rhinoceros becomes relevant. The German pre-Nazi government decided that they would rather have this print as exemplar of a species than an accurate picture of the real thing. It is a very Nazi sort of decision, choosing a leading Germanic artist for ideological reasons to include in books about facts, when the facts are not sufficiently self-promoting.

If you can eliminate bodies of knowledge, the compendia housed in libraries of the predigital era, where access to physical tomes was required to look up facts, then you can rewrite facts as you see fit. That was what Nazi book theft was about. The ability to manipulate history, and therefore program the thoughts of future generations, is far more valuable than the auction price of a painting. But it requires a colossal-scale operation, sweeping libraries clean, because "real" history books lurking here and there would be like time bombs—future scholars might find them and question your tailored version of reality. Thus it is not outrageous to see the Nazis' attempt at wiping history clean by stripping Europe of its books as analogous to attempts to physically wipe Europe clean of what the Nazis considered "lesser" races. They are part and parcel and, as Rydell argues, they are also chicken and egg.

Today, information remains in books, and that information tends to be deemed most reliable. Presumably one or more editors and fact-checkers examined the material, and particularly in scholarly works with citations, the content of these tomes is likely to be accurate to the best knowledge of contemporary researchers. But still, searching for answers in libraries and books is limited to but one subsection of the world's population: students and professors and scientists and the odd intellectually rigorous layman. Most folks go online for "facts" and read sites like Wikipedia, which anyone can alter (for better or worse). A contemporary version of the Nazi book theft would be if, say, some presidential candidate, in league with some superpower in opposition to the country for which that candidate was running for office, were to somehow take over the entire Internet and erase fact-based pages, in order to replace them, later on, with histories of their choosing. After a generation or so, the world might forget how history had been presented before and learn only this newly imposed version of events. Logistically, a cyber-conspiracy of that sort would be easier to pull off than seizing every single book across an entire continent.

Among many proper photographs, you can still find Dürer's print on the Wikipedia page for "rhinoceros." If one day the photographs vanish, and we're left only with a single, ideologically chosen exemplar (no matter how beautiful), then it's time to start worrying.

Looted Antiquities

It is unfortunately a well-known fact that the art trade has occasionally been infiltrated by unscrupulous characters—art forgers, flippers, and thieves are among the first to come to mind. In modern art history, the cases of outright art theft are rare and newsworthy. But in the antiquities trade, theft is more complicated, and in some ways, more common. Looted antiquities taken from sites of discovery before they can be recorded are able to enter the market and be sold at something approaching their full value—unheard of for an item stolen from a museum and traded in back rooms. Indeed, deals for objects purloined from the field are made, all too often, out in the open at art fairs.

A gallery that has been involved in selling looted antiquities in the past participated in the 2018 Salon Art + Design Fair in New York City. Based in Geneva and New York, Phoenix Ancient Art has sold to major museums and collectors the world over, including the Metropolitan Museum of Art. But as the *New York Times* and other publications have profiled, they've also been involved in several cases where the pieces they were selling turned out to be stolen or looted. These involved an ancient Egyptian stele, and an Iranian drinking vessel that was illegally imported and had been taken from an Iranian cave.

With this in mind, the question easily becomes: What kind of responsibility should fair organizers have to protect the buyers? It would be discriminatory for a fair to restrict the inclusion of a dealer because of past issues and bad press, but at the same time, buyers will assume that fairs are curated to some extent, and that those selling there have been screened by the organizers, and even perhaps that they can shop without worry. In fact, most fairs charge for galleries to exhibit and sell in them, and so there is a financial disincentive to be choosy about who shows.

For buyers, the safest bet, in this time of conflict zones in the Middle East, is to not buy anything that seems to come from the countries caught up in turmoil, unless it has very elaborate and overt documentation that shows that it has been in collections for many decades and was legally excavated and exported. The safest of all is a moratorium on buying antiquities from these locations, period, but that is not logistically feasible, as it would grind a section of the art trade to a halt. And beyond that, ensuring that the gallery you purchased from has checked the item against registries for stolen artwork is also a must. But even that has its issues.

Phoenix Ancient Art proved due diligence in the case of the Egyptian stele, because they did check to ensure it was not on a stolen art database. And herein lies the reason why the antiquities market has an entirely different problem to those trading in art sales. The stele would never have appeared on a stolen art database, because it was plucked from the earth, not from an extant collection.

Ultimately, the solution should come back to law enforcement. Getting into trouble for having acquired a looted antiquity does not happen as often as would be necessary to really curb the problem. Private collectors will frequently get off the hook by proving due diligence (having checked with police and databases to ensure that the object did not appear) and good faith (that you genuinely believed the object was legitimate when you bought it).

As Lynda Albertson, CEO of ARCA, told the *Observer*, "Legal seizures, like those recently filed in New York State court and in London, provide one of the strongest disincentives yet to dealing in or purchasing looted cultural objects without sufficient due diligence." And she noted, "Buying and selling illicit objects defrauds the legitimate trade in works of ancient art, but more than that, it corrupts our understanding of history." There must be more such seizures—it must feel like capture is a high probability—in order for trading in ill-gotten goods to become a consistent liability.

So ultimately, no, the responsibility should not be on the part of fairs to police what is being sold under their roofs. What is actually required is an overhaul to the system of buying antiquities, which currently only asks that the buyer passively demonstrate that they did not realize that it was looted. Instead, the best solution would be to require the middleman and the ultimate buyer to proactively show that the activity is legitimate through documentation. Failure to do that would result in legal action, and the uptick in policing would indeed cause many dealers to think twice before passing along something with sketchy provenance.

But doing so would be such a sea change, and would surely cause outcry from the world of art trading, that it seems an impossibility. It would require a truly worldwide legislation to shift in this direction, otherwise the trade would just move operations to a less legally cumbersome country.

Are Major Mafias Really behind Many Art Thefts?

Caravaggio's *Nativity*, stolen from the church of San Lorenzo in Palermo on October 18, 1969, and still missing, may be one step closer to recovery. Taken by members of Cosa Nostra, the Sicilian Mafia, during a time when Italy was cracking down on organized crime, its theft prompted the establishment of the world's first dedicated art police unit, the Italian Carabinieri Division for the Protection of Cultural Heritage. But the painting has not been seen since.

The general rule is that famous art is not stolen for display at some supervillain's lair. That is largely a myth promoted in film and fiction (including one of my own books, I'm afraid, *The Art Thief*). What happens to most famous stolen art is more complicated, but also in many ways more interesting. Simply selling it is supremely difficult, and when attempts to do so are made, the result is often a slip-up by the crooks and the recovery of the art by police. With this in mind, some stolen art enters a closed black market, used as barter or collateral in deals with other organized crime groups for other illicit goods. But there are some prominent exceptions to this rule, and the fate of this Caravaggio may be one of them.

Journalist Peter Watson went undercover for the Carabinieri to try to recover the work in 1979, pretending to be a shifty art collector (he wrote of this adventure in *The Caravaggio Conspiracy*). Police often learn who was behind thefts through a paid network of criminal informants. The Carabinieri had learned that Cosa Nostra members were boasting possession of the painting, and Watson was recruited to lure them into offering it to him. He concluded that Cosa Nostra was indeed very likely in possession of the Caravaggio, but he was not offered it for sale—instead he was offered a Bronzino and an Andrea del Sarto, which were recovered through this sting operation.

In 1996, a Mafia *penitento*, an informant, claimed that he had stolen the Caravaggio back in 1979 on the request of a high-ranking boss. In 2009, another *penitento* asked about the Caravaggio said that he'd heard, back in 1999, that the painting had been ruined during an earthquake while in storage in Sicily and had subsequently been eaten by rats and pigs rooting through the rubble. The work is still number one on the FBI's Most Wanted Stolen Works of Art list, but it has since been labeled "missing, presumed destroyed."

But new hope recently dawned on the horizon. Yet another *penitento* has claimed to the Carabinieri that the Caravaggio remained intact and was acquired by a Mafia boss, Gaetano Badalamenti, who was in touch with an art dealer in Switzerland prior to his arrest in 1984. The head of Italy's anti-Mafia unit announced last week that there was "enough evidence to launch a new investigation," with a focus on Switzerland. So it is entirely possible that the painting has survived its kidnap by Cosa Nostra and can be found again. And just maybe it is one of those cinema-style exceptions, and sat for decades on a mob boss's wall?

This is just one of the many stories of major mafias involved in art theft, and the one with the freshest and most promising update. The history of major international criminal syndicates involvement in art crime dates back to the 1960s, when the Unione Corse, or Corsican Mafia, based in Marseille, was responsible for a series of art thefts along the French Riviera during the 1960s and '70s, including heists of paintings from the renowned restaurant Le Colombe d'Or, from the home of art dealer Armand Dronant, and culminating with the theft of 118 Picassos from a special exhibit at the Papal Palace in Avignon.

As described in an article I wrote for the Spring 2012 issue of the *Journal of Art Crime*, the Corsican Mafia's interest in obtaining art (by whatever means necessary) was almost certainly prompted by the parallel burgeoning of interest by the media in the extraordinary prices for which art was selling at auction. In 1961, world-record prices were recorded for the sale of Picasso and Cezanne paintings, and Sotheby's sale of Rembrandt's *Aristotle Contemplating a Bust of Homer* for $2.3 million also set an auction record. These were reported in newspapers and on television. To a major international organized crime syndicate, these high-value paintings looked simply like easily portable, relatively underprotected, expensive objects. Unsurprisingly, the Corsican Mafia began to steal exactly what they had read was of value in news reports: particularly Cezanne and Picasso paintings. The Corsican Mafia brought with them the techniques that had proven successful in past criminal enterprises, namely the threat of violence. Guards at the Papal Palace in Avignon were bound and gagged and threatened with beatings, as members of the Mafia made off with their astonishing haul of Picassos.

But it seems that while the thieves recognized that it would not be all that difficult to steal these famous paintings and drawings, they were not certain as to how they could be sold. Within days of this theft, all but one of the Picassos was recovered and arrests were made—the Mafia hadn't yet worked out what to do with the freshly stolen art, but the learning curve would be quick.

Art police say that most art crime, since the 1960s, has involved organized crime at some point in the life of the crime (theft, smuggling, laundering, fencing, etc.), and this definition includes both smaller groups who work together in criminal enterprises for collective, long-term goals (as opposed to quick cash crimes) and large criminal syndicates, or "mafias." Such major syndicates have been involved in innumerable high-profile art crimes, several of which we will discuss below, from the Corsican Mafia's rash of thefts along the French Riviera in the 1960s and '70s to the Russian Mafia's involvement in several thefts of Edvard Munch paintings, to the Balkan Mafia's role in art thefts in Zürich, such as the 2008 heist from the Bührle collection, to Cosa Nostra's famous 1969 theft of Caravaggio's *Nativity*. But it is not always, or even often, clear who is behind art heists. Deep knowledge of crimes only tends to come when a crime is solved and criminals prosecuted—the court record reveals the details that help us understand what happened. But law enforcement the world over is pretty bad at prosecuting art crime. As noted in my book *The Museum of Lost Art*, as little as 1.5 percent of art theft cases end with the recovery of the object and successful prosecution of the criminals. Police learn who is, or which groups are, behind thefts through criminal informants, but such information must be taken with a grain of salt. Which Mafia *penitento* is telling the truth about the Caravaggio *Nativity*?

This case exemplifies how larger organized crime syndicates like Cosa Nostra acquire stolen art and also try to sell that art to potential buyers who are "screened" ahead of time to ensure that they are not police in disguise. In this case, the Carabinieri helped build an identity and history for Peter Watson that suggested that he was a legitimate art dealer who was not afraid to buy questionable pieces. Known art dealers and art world personalities contributed to this subterfuge, providing documents, letters, contracts, and so on, which would give the impression that Watson's character had a long career as a dealer.

They must have done the job well. The representatives of Cosa Nostra failed to detect his undercover status. They also may have been eager to believe that Watson was legitimate; criminals are clearly under the impression that there's a market out there for stolen art, otherwise would they be making these thefts at all? But did they get this impression from experience or assumption? There is a market out there for stolen work, but connecting with such individuals can be difficult, even for criminals with an elaborate international network at their disposal. Watson's experience speaks to this difficulty, too, because if said criminal collectors were easy to find, the stolen art would have already been sold, or Watson would have been asked to bid against other potential buyers in the closed black market of stolen art. Criminals seem to believe that they can find Dr. No/Thomas Crown criminal art collector types as seen in films. But there are precious few such figures in confirmed historical case studies, and the fact that criminals fall for police in disguise confirms that such exotic characters almost exclusively roam the realm of fiction.

But this also speaks to the fact that resale isn't the only reason the Mafia has been involved in art theft. Their other manner of using stolen art is harder to stop, because it involves a closed circle of deals among criminal groups. As in the case of a 1986 theft by Martin Cahill, head of an Irish organized crime group, of eighteen artworks from Russborough House, stolen art is used as collateral on loans and in a barter system for other illicit goods. As I outlined in my 2016 book, *Art Crime: Terrorists, Tomb Raiders, Forgers and Thieves*, a Vermeer taken by Cahill was smuggled to Antwerp where it was used as collateral on a loan. A Gabriël Metsu painting also taken then was recovered in Turkey being swapped for a shipment of heroin. Thus, art stolen from extant collections can provide a variety of benefits for major organized crime groups.

Dealing in looted antiquities, objects taken directly and clandestinely out of the earth, is a far easier way that crime syndicates have found to profit. Paolo Giorgio Ferri, a leading Italian attorney who prosecuted the infamous antiquities looting ringleader Giacomo Medici, estimates that 90 percent of all antiquities looting is undertaken by groups involved in organized crime (as opposed to individuals or smaller groups interested in short-term cash only, not in collective, long-term goals, as are organized criminal groups). The loss of archaeological context then becomes one among many problems, as the looted antiquities fund all manner of other activities in which organized crime is involved. As he explained at a recent ARCA Conference on Art Crime, objects taken directly out of the earth have never been seen by modern eyes and will never appear on any stolen art database; thus they can be sold openly, at full value, if accompanied by a false paper trail suggesting that they were legally excavated and exported.

Some cases offer surprise connections to major mafias and fuel the popular misconception that most stolen art ends up at the home of Dr. Nos. The theft of two Van Gogh paintings, *View of the Sea at Scheveningen* and *Congregation Leaving the Reformed Church in Nuenen*, from Amsterdam's Van Gogh Museum on December 7, 2002, remained a mystery for more than a decade, with no promising leads on recovering the art. It came as a surprise when, in September 2016, Italian police involved in an unrelated raid on the holiday home of a member of the Camorra, the Campanian Mafia, spotted the two Van Goghs hanging on the wall. Well, maybe not such a big surprise, after all. There must be, or must have been, organized crime bosses willing to buy stolen art, or even commissioning the theft of art, a la Dr. No. The stolen Van Goghs, likely the Caravaggio *Nativity*, and some other high-profile cases spark the idea of the criminal art collector. But such verified examples are few and far between. Were criminal art collectors easier to find if they did not or have never existed, then criminals wouldn't fall for undercover operators posing as such, a la Peter Watson in disguise. But they likewise must be rare and difficult to find, or else clever criminals would not become desperate enough to fall for someone like Peter Watson. If there was any doubt that stolen art sometimes ends up on criminal boss's walls, then pleasant surprises, like the 2016 Van Gogh painting recovery, offer sufficient evidence to put doubts to rest—and perhaps to suggest where other objects among the tens of thousands reported stolen each year to Interpol might be found.

Are the Swedish Crown Jewel Thieves Fools or Geniuses?

On July 30, 2018, a pair of thieves swiped a king's ransom of treasures from their display case at Strängnäs Cathedral in Sweden. The seventeenth-century Swedish royal crown jewels, including a scepter, crowns, and an orb made of gold and bedecked with precious gems, used by King Charles IX, were ferried off by speedboat. In a cinematic twist, the boat was chased by police in helicopters, boats, and cars but managed to escape in the labyrinth that is the Swedish coast, pocked with islands and tributaries.

A theft of such filmic ingenuity seems to suggest ingenious thieves. But then on February 5, those same crown jewels were found by a security guard in a plastic bag, atop a garbage can in a suburb of Stockholm.

This rediscovery coincides with the trial of the only suspect arrested in conjunction with the theft, a twenty-two-year-old man who denies involvement in the crown jewel heist but admitted to having stolen a bicycle and the speedboat used in the heist.

If this were not intriguing, and confounding enough, just a few years prior, in 2013, a different set of Swedish crown jewels, those of King Johan III, were stolen, only to be found in a garbage bag left on the shoulder of a highway, after an anonymous tip was called in to the police.

What are we dealing with? Much of the media response has been to suggest two things: that it is all too easy to steal cultural heritage objects, and that the thieves can't figure out what to do with such "hot" art once they have it, so they simply give up and abandon it.

Perhaps. There are certainly numerous historical precedents to suggest as much. Consider the 2003 theft from the Whitworth Gallery in Manchester, United Kingdom. Three paintings, by Van Gogh, Picasso, and Gauguin, were stolen, only to be returned shortly thereafter, found rolled in a tube outside a public lavatory in a park near the gallery. Some said that the theft was a prank to expose the poor security of the museum, but it is more likely that it was an excuse made after having failed to come up with a plan to profit from the stolen goods.

There's a very famous case study in point. When Vincenzo Peruggia stole the *Mona Lisa* in 1911, he at least thought about seeking a buyer. A list of wealthy art collectors, many American, was found among his possessions. But he likely (and correctly) concluded that it was implausible that he, a destitute Italian handyman living in squalor in Paris, could reach them to make a deal. Instead he kept the painting in his apartment for years, before smuggling it to Italy in order to gift it to the Uffizi, claiming that his only desire was to right the historical wrong and return an Italian masterpiece that, he believed, had been looted by Napoleon (it hadn't been—it was bought legally from Leonardo's inheritors by King Francois I, but it was a fair guess, as Napoleon had looted tens of thousands of artworks from Italy).

The 2004 theft of two paintings by Edvard Munch, a version of *The Scream* and *Madonna*, from the Munch Museum in Oslo resulted in a protracted attempt on the part of the criminals to extract ransom. Failing to do so, they just abandoned the paintings in a car parked on a farm outside of Oslo. But in a parallel case, four paintings were stolen in 2008 from the Bührle collection in Zürich. Two of them, both by Monet, were found a few days later in an unlocked car parked in front of a mental hospital a few hundred yards away from the victimized museum. This case differed from the Munch story in that the recovery of two of the paintings took place so quickly after the theft that it suggests either absolute ineptitude or clever proactivity on the part of the criminals. Were they so foolish, as some reports suggested, to accidentally leave their hard-stolen-art to be picked up again? A little logic suggests otherwise.

In many of the world's countries, including the United Kingdom, it is illegal to pay a ransom to criminals. Whether to rescue a kidnapped person or an object, this is illegal because paying a ransom encourages future such kidnappings. Consider a case at the Museum of Modern Art in Milan—five paintings were stolen, a ransom was paid, and they were returned . . . only for the exact same paintings to be stolen again, and never recovered. That is why it is not recommended to pay ransom.

But ransoms sometimes are paid, just in an under-the-table manner. This was almost certainly the case (though its factuality was never made public) in the Bührle Museum case. Two of the paintings were returned by the criminals intentionally, likely after a ransom was paid, by leaving them in the car parked across from the museum. This is the most probable explanation also for both Swedish crown jewels recoveries. The 2013 loot was returned in a manner designed to make it easy to retrieve by authorities without endangering the criminals, likely after a ransom was paid that was never made public. And the most recent recovery? The fact that the goods resurfaced just as the only apprehended suspect went on trial is beyond plausible coincidence. It sounds precisely like a plea bargain: return the goods for a lesser sentence.

Sometimes criminals can demonstrate their foolishness through seemingly foolish actions. But there is often method to their madness.

Ten Cost-Effective Steps to Improve Security at Your Museum

In the wonderful Arms and Armor collection of the Philadelphia Museum of Art, there stands a medieval sword, made in Europe in the first half of the fourteenth century, and likely seized from a fallen Crusader knight by Islamic soldiers. The sword is in immaculate condition and retains its original wooden handle, thanks to its preservation in a Mamluk armory in Alexandria since its original capture. Its blade is inscribed with an Arabic phrase which includes the following warning notice: "Whomever shall seize [this sword] and not return it shall commit a crime."

Fear of art theft, even when the artwork is in the form of a functional weapon, has been present throughout history. From Albrecht Dürer's copyright warning to potential forgers in 1506 that he and his patron would fiercely prosecute any would-be Renaissance copyists of his prints, to the carving on this sword blade, art security has been a constant concern.

Despite this, a great many of the world's museums remain underprotected, often loath to alter or update their security plans for a variety of reasons, from pleading poverty to simple inertia to restrictions placed by donors and insurers. As the director of a major Venetian collection once told me, "We have very few security measures in place, because nothing has ever been stolen from our museum. Why would we spend money to fix what's never been broken?" The answer to this is that the good fortune of never having been burgled is no excuse for stasis, because the update of security measures post-theft is closing the barn door after the cows have left.

Art museums have never been as well nor as expensively secured. And yet, museum theft is rising. Why this discrepancy? The answer comes when we examine when museum thefts are taking place. Criminals now shy away from thefts during hours of closure, when a museum can batten down the hatches and huddle inside a protective shell of locks and alarms. But the inherent difficulty in museum security is that during open hours one must provide comfortable access to museumgoers, while at the same time maintaining a controlled security risk situation. Criminals have turned their attention to daytime thefts during open hours, when the museum is full of tourists and vulnerable to surprise thefts. Recent dramatic examples of "blitz" thefts, armed masked criminals running into museums, waving guns, and running out, have occurred at the Bührle collection, the Munch Museum, and the Stockholm Museum of Art, among countless others. Alarms go off as they are meant to, but average police response time in most cities is three to five minutes. If the thieves are in and out in under three minutes, then the alarms are nothing more than a noise box, summoning help that arrives after the thieves have left, carrying the "cows" under their arms.

Based on an extensive analysis of how thieves and vandals have historically succeeded in stealing or damaging art in museums, ARCA is pleased to present ten general suggestions, adaptable to any museum worldwide, that would significantly improve security at no or minimal additional cost. Every museum is different, and part of a good security plan is to tailor any suggestions to each museum and to each room and object within that collection. Anyone who suggests that there is a single, universal solution to art security has already proven their inexperience. But the following are adaptable and work within the normal existing structure of most museum security. Without spending thousands (or sometimes millions) on hi-tech security, museums worldwide could be strengthened, preventing theft and vandalism with minimal imposition on the status quo. The result will be a happier, more focused, and more effective security force—a strong deterrent to potential criminals.

1. Guards Greet Guests

Human security guards are, historically, the least-effective line of defense in art museums. And yet, they are potentially the most valuable commodity. The key to this new approach to museum security is a shift in expected habits of museum guards, in order to improve the morale, interest, and focus in a profession which might see ten or twenty years of service without a single genuine threat situation. How do you transform a potentially boring, repetitive occupation into something fun and therefore demanding of pleasurable focus? It is human nature to "switch off" if one's occupation is something passive. How often have we seen museum guards finishing a crossword puzzle or catching up on a good book? So the key, at no extra cost, is to make a game out of museum security—but one which results in an increasingly effective staff.

One easy step is to ask guards to greet every guest who walks past them. Make eye contact, smile, and say "hello" and "welcome." Interact with guests, ask if they need directions should they look lost (or should they look above or behind artworks, which may indicate hostile surveillance). This greeting prompts guards to focus on each guest (see the next suggestion for more on this) and makes each guest aware that they are being surveyed. For guests with a clean conscience, this will seem friendly and helpful. For those up to no good, this will discomfit them. The key follow-up is for guards to monitor the reactions from museum guests immediately after being greeted. Comfortable guests will continue normally. But if a guest suddenly becomes nervous, or hightails it out of the room, then it suggests that they were frightened by the attention of the friendly security guard and their further actions should be monitored.

It is up to each security director as to what the preferred follow-up reaction might be, should a guest exhibit some suspicious signs. We recommend that the guard notify central security, and then follow up the initial greeting with one more interaction. A guilty party will be dissuaded from further action by this security attention, while the innocent will find it helpful and friendly.

2. Evaluate Signs

Humans tend to exhibit one or more from among a series of physiological characteristics of nervousness. These range from the entirely obvious and overt (quickening breath, sweaty palms, thirst, feeling of tightness around the collar) to the more subtle (quick eye movements, deep breaths to regain focus, clearing the throat, looking behind their back). Based on the work of dear friends of ARCA Dick Drent of the Van Gogh Museum and Anthony Amore of the Gardner Museum (whose plan was inspired by his time leading Homeland Security at Logan Airport, during which he consulted with Israeli counterintelligence agents), museums are encouraged to develop a roster of telltale signs that guards can look for, an accumulation of which suggest that the subject surveyed is, to put it in simple terms, "up to no good." This technique is used by security in airports to scan travelers for potential terrorists. Those exhibiting multiple signs of nervousness are elevated to a higher level of security control (for instance, their bag might be searched by hand). A similar format should be used in museums—if guards read several signs of nervousness in a guest, they should approach them in a friendly and helpful manner and ask if the guest needs help, directions to a water fountain, if it's too warm in the gallery, and so on. Once again, this will be seen as helpful by innocent guests and will intimidate those with a guilty conscience. It also provides guards with a proactive "game" to play—looking for set characteristics in each museumgoer, playing the role of profiler. Allowing the guards themselves to follow up their surveillance and interact with the guests also empowers them, and breaks the repetitive, passive nature of the work of guarding.

3. Curate At-Risk Objects Together in a Defensible Location

Although curators may bridle at this idea, objects considered to be high-risk, particularly for vandalism, should be clustered together in an easily defended location, flanked by extra security guards. They should be as far as possible from entrances and exits, approachable from as few angles as possible, and a guard should be stationed so that their presence may be felt by museumgoers. This physical presence will be a deterrent to vandals, who might foresee that they would be intercepted before their successful attack (a key point because most vandals do not mind if they are arrested after the successful attack). At-risk objects for vandalism include famous objects, those recently featured in the media, but also unusual interpretations of religious themes, and sexually charged or sexually questionable works, particularly when those works are hybridized with religious themes.

4. Notice of CCTV, but Keep Cameras Hidden

As Michel Foucault's book *Discipline and Punish* tells us, surveillance and the fear of surveillance is the prime crime deterrent in modern society. But the presence of surveillance equipment and alarms is only a deterrent if the equipment cannot be seen and therefore cannot be plotted against through hostile surveillance. It is a given that museums will have cameras and alarms (although a surprising number do not)—and criminals will visit museums to engage in hostile surveillance, locating security equipment in order to plot ways around it. If it is made known that the security equipment is in use, but if it is hidden and cannot be seen by museumgoers, it will disconcert hostile surveyors and dissuade them from entering into a plan with unknown variables. This runs against the more common rationale of placing surveillance equipment in obvious locations to reinforce to visitors that they are being surveyed. For criminals "casing" a potential target, seeing the equipment will facilitate their sense of comfort and understanding of the target location. Deprive them of that comfort by hiding security equipment, but letting them know, nonetheless, that it is present and active.

5. Airport-Style Security (or an Equivalent) at the Entrance, Exit Rotating Doors

It is expensive, and somewhat unwieldy, to install airport-style security (single-file lines, mandatory metal detection, bags go through an X-ray machine and must be checked, etc.) at the entrance to museums. It is certainly the best guarantee against vandalism (protecting against metal entering the museum) and it is the only certain guarantee against the recent trend in smash-and-grab blitz thefts, for the simple reason that it clogs the entrance with equipment, security guards, and museumgoers. If installing this system is not feasible, then some equivalent should be devised, narrowing the entrance to one door through which each entrant may be observed by security guards—and through which visitors can see that they are being observed by security guards. The narrowing of the entrance, a security trick that dates back to early fortification and castle design, will control the flow of visitors entering the museum, give security a chance to profile them as they enter, clog up the entrance to prevent blitz thefts, and allow visitors to see the strong security measures in place.

As with the entrance, the exit points should be controlled. Guards should be stationed at the exits, which should ideally be single file, allowing the guards to clearly see each visitor (and what they are carrying) as they exit. The ideal door type is a rotating door which can be locked suddenly at the push of a button. This permits maximum control and observation at the exit point and minimizes the chance that someone can leave with a stolen object.

6. Work with Local Police

Police response time is one of the largest factors that aids thieves in the recent trend of blitz thefts. By the same token, museum guards should not be expected to respond to armed assaults and should never be armed themselves (a theft that turns into a firefight in a room full of tourists, or a potential hostage situation, is in no one's interest). Security should work with local police so that they feel they are all on the same "team," there to protect property. Ideally, local police would be stationed or patrol near the museum during open hours. A local police presence, overt and alert, will deter potential criminals and also minimize response time in the event of an alarm.

7. Combine Low- and Hi-Tech Security

Particularly in the United States, trustees and insurers tend to insist on hi-tech, expensive security measures, assuming that the more something costs to defend, the safer it will be. But the history of art theft is full of ridiculous security gaffs, most the fault of technology failures. Museums can be victimized because of their overreliance on technology. A good way to counteract this is to combine low-tech and hi-tech security measures in any one museum, and indeed in any one gallery. No museum should have one, universal security method—because if it is breached, everything is vulnerable. Rather, defend different objects in different ways, ranging from laser alarms to high-tensile steel fishing line, emphasizing creativity and surprise—the best ways to counter hostile surveillance. Rotate the manner in which objects are protected at irregular intervals. Once again, if criminals are discomfited, not permitted success in their hostile surveillance, then they will be unlikely to follow through with a theft from this shrouded target.

8. Promotion and Awards for Staff

Borrow from the McDonald's approach to encouraging staff, and incorporate promotions and awards for diligence among security staff. Inserting elevated positions of responsibility (not necessarily coupled with pay raises), and awarding staff for particular diligence, will be a great motivator, and motivated workers will work better and more effectively.

9. Art and Art Crime Talks for Staff

There is often a schism in museums between curators and staff, particularly security. This is unfortunate, because when it comes down to it, all are working toward the same goal—protecting the art while displaying it. Encourage intermingling of staff and curators, and praise or award security staff who attend talks on the art under their protection. This will empower security staff, give them a sense that they are a team that understands the value of what they protect. Talks on art crime, too, will improve the depth and knowledge of the staff, and give them the chance to think for themselves about ways to improve security and their own effectiveness.

10. Interview Your Staff Before and After Employment

A significant percentage of museum thefts are the result of some insider connection, often in the form of information provided to criminals by disgruntled former staff. To prevent this, careful interviews must be made of prospective security staff, even if they are provided by a known external security company. Insist on criminal record checks for all staff—if they object, do not hire them, as it means they have something to hide. Critically, conduct exit interviews of all staff leaving the museum. Ask questions subtly designed to determine whether there is any ill feeling in the leaving staff for the museum. Upon leaving, certain security measures should be altered, to safeguard against the usefulness of the sale of insider information.

The Iceberg of Looted Art: A Glimpse of the Gurlitt Hoard

I was seated behind the desk long used by Jože Plečnik, the Slovenian modernist architect about whom I'd written my doctoral dissertation, which has just been published as a book. I was filming a tie-in documentary for Slovenian national television, about to tell the camera about Plečnik's home, which is now an award-winning museum in Ljubljana. My eyes drifted over the books on one end of the great man's desk, and I did a cartoon double-take that required a "cut" from the director and a retake. What had distracted me was the name on the cover of an old book, one that the curators had left on the desk, as if Plečnik had just been reading it and slipped out for a cup of tea. The author's name was Gurlitt.

This was Hildebrand Gurlitt, the well-respected scholar of art history (well respected in terms of scholarship, not for his Nazi sympathies). Tagged as "Hitler's Art Thief" in the title of a 2015 book (there are several people who could bear that damning title), he is the father of Cornelius Gurlitt, inheritor of the art that Hildebrand bought at scandalously cut prices (mostly from fleeing and pressurized Jewish owners) or siphoned off (few details are yet known about the stories behind these artworks, though a team of researchers is hard at work). An exhibit at the Kunstmuseum in Bern, Switzerland, opens November 2 and another exhibit opens November 3, 2017, at the in Bundeskunsthalle in Bonn, Germany.

For the first time, objects seized from the Gurlitt hoard were displayed to the public, as part of the preamble to these major exhibitions.

When, in 2012, Cornelius was investigated for tax evasion, his Munich-area apartment was opened and found to be packed with lost art—1,406 works, to be precise, including pieces by Matisse, Chagall, Dix, Renoir, and Monet.

After his death in 2014, Gurlitt bequeathed these works to the Kunstmuseum in Bern (an interesting choice, perhaps, to move the works outside of Germany, to Switzerland, where they would be less associated with Nazi loot, or possibly because of a grudge against the German state). After much debate in the media about the morality of accepting a gift of looted art, the museum decided to take the bequeathal, provided nothing was contested by a past owner. (Several works were; they were returned, and the museum is cooperating with any future claims, as it is anticipated that there will be many such claims.) This sort of unlikely motherlode offers hope that other such hidden treasuries of vanished works might still be out there. It is merely the tip of the looted art iceberg.

Every lost artwork tells a story. The Gurlitt hoard ("hoard" is preferred to "collection," as one wouldn't wish to overdignify the looting) contains some 1,406 stories (though the exact number of objects seized from various Gurlitt properties is unclear). The biographies of these artworks, each having survived decades, if not centuries, of tumult, makes for reading as fascinating as the memoir of any once-living being. But what haunts are the remaining question marks, the works that may have been destroyed, may have been saved, may be lost forever, or may turn up in some future Gurlitt-like cache of treasures.

Much of the Gurlitt stash was thought to have been purchased by Hildebrand during the Second World War from Jewish families, who sold them to provide escape routes. While not part of the Gurlitt discovery, this was the case for an ethereal painting by Gustav Klimt, *Portrait of Trude Steiner*, an early work from around 1900, before Klimt became the toast of Viennese society.

Jenny Steiner, mother of the girl portrayed, fled Vienna in 1938, just after the Nazis took control of the city. The Nazis seized the painting from her, ostensibly in lieu of missing tax payments, though there is no record of whether the Steiners indeed owed anything, and it is unlikely that they did. Such pretenses were a common Nazi tactic to take things that they had targeted. The painting's path after seizure is cloudy, but it was sold at auction in April 1941, and it has not been seen since. This ghost of a painting, now there, now gone, is all the more haunting as it was a posthumous portrait of young Trude, shown aged thirteen. A ghost of a ghost.

The collection of Serena Lederer (Jenny Steiner's sister, both of them née Pulitzer and relatives of Joseph Pulitzer, after whom the literary prize was named) contained many works by Klimt, all of which were confiscated by the Nazis when she fled Vienna for Budapest in 1940, hoping to remain just ahead of the Nazi tide. The Gestapo packed up her family collection and moved it to a looted art storehouse, Immendorf Castle, one of many such treasuries where Nazis planned to store valuables until the war's end.

For the vast quantities of art that have changed hands in war (in the Second World War alone, some estimates suggest that five million cultural heritage objects changed hands inappropriately), hope remains because of the obvious value of most of the objects involved. Though it may not seem like it at first, the discovery of the Gurlitt hoard in 2012 was one of the best pieces of news to strike the art world. That so many tens of thousands of artworks went missing is, of course, tragic. But if 1,406 can be found in a single apartment, then we might maintain a modicum of optimism that other stashes of lost treasures may surface, other Gurlitt-like hoards, small and large.

On May 8, 1945, the SS set fire to Immendorf Castle, probably destroying all of its contents—though a glimmer of hope remains that some of the objects, like the *Portrait of Trude Steiner*, might have been spirited out before the flames swallowed them.

Objects of evident value are more likely to be preserved, in any circumstance, and there is benefit to no one (aside from iconoclasts) for artworks to be destroyed or damaged or left to decay. So perhaps some of the works now labeled as lost, but almost certainly destroyed, like the Klimts from Schloss Immendorf, were in fact saved? And perhaps time and circumstance will peel back locked doors and sealed attics, and other caches of lost art will come to light?

The Maltese Priest and the Kidnapped Caravaggio

On December 29, 1984, three people dressed as workmen strolled into a cathedral in Malta and robbed it of a Caravaggio. They strung a "Work in Progress" sign over the entrance to the cathedral of St. John in Valletta, lowered the hefty painting, *Saint Jerome*, in its gilt frame, and then roughly cut it out. "An American tourist complained the church was closed," says Father Marius Zerafa, recalling the incident. "When the curator came to see what the fuss was about, he got the shock of his life!"

Father Zerafa is a sprightly eighty-seven-year-old (he passed away in 2022, several years after this essay was written), and he's lived a full life ripe with art—the pipe-smoking Dominican priest and painter eventually became director of all of Malta's museums—but the most dramatic episode of his career was beating this gang of criminals to get that Caravaggio back.

Two years passed with no leads on the painting, which shows the elderly saint writing his famous translation of the New Testament, the first in Latin, called the Vulgate. In that time, the thieves smuggled it to Florence but failed to find a buyer—they even offered it to auction houses. The vast majority of stolen artworks are never recovered (as few as 2 to 6 percent in most cases), so the outlook for its recovery was bleak. But desperate to profit from their hard-stolen trophy, the thieves decided to ransom it back to the cathedral, via Father Zerafa.

Zerafa was born into an influential Maltese family (his uncle, Sir Paul Boffa, became prime minister in 1947) and despite being "not particularly pious," he joined the Dominican monastic order, aged sixteen, impressed by the riveting sermons of a priest who would later be canonized. He spent his first three years in his native Malta, before moving to Staffordshire and Oxford, where he stayed until 1952. He studied art history at University of London and La Sorbonne. Back home in Malta, he became curator and then director of the museums of Malta.

On November 24, 1986, a young man approached Zerafa and thrust him an envelope containing a cassette and a Polaroid. He said the envelope was from Joe Borg, a very common name in Malta. Zerafa didn't ask any questions—he assumed it was from his cousin of the same name. But the Polaroid was a recent shot of the Caravaggio, and the tape contained careful instructions from the thieves. "They gave me a password and instructed me not to speak to the police," he says. "They wanted a ransom of half a million Maltese lire."

As Malta's leading art historian, he was something of a celebrity—a vivacious, outspoken priest and professor, always grinning, often appearing on television. He was the obvious person to contact for the ransom demand.

Because of police corruption scandals in the early eighties, Zerafa was worried the thieves had police contacts: the man on the tape said the criminals would know immediately if the police were involved. He resisted telling the police but did divulge the ransom demand to his bishop and Malta's cultural minister, neither of whom had any intention of paying up, so as not to encourage future such art-napping. "Their reaction was not encouraging at all," Zerafa says. "Ministers aren't really interested in art. In my twenty years at the museums of Malta, I've learnt that a minister only attends a show if he's the prime exhibit. At times, it was easier to deal with the Mafia than with ministers and monsignori."

The thieves got impatient. They began to call daily. After weeks and no money changing hands, Zerafa got a parcel in the post, containing a slice of the Caravaggio canvas. They would slice off strips until they were paid, or the painting was destroyed. "When I received the first strip I was really happy, because I knew there was still a chance of getting it back. It had a special kind of lining, so I told the minister I would swear it was ours." Though he did not have access to the money, Zerafa feigned a serious interest in paying the ransom, to stop the thieves from damaging the work further. He argued he could not raise half a million but could get a quarter of a million.

Then the frequent phone calls from the nervous thieves gave him an idea. He consulted a retired Carabinieri art detective and set up his own sting operation, with a young colleague who traced the phone calls to a small footwear factory. Father Zerafa traveled to the town and made inquiries, via a wily taxi driver, to find out about the factory. "Every worker in Malta has a small booklet with his photo, name, details, called a workbook. They're kept at the ministry. I asked to look at them and got to know that there were four men working at the shoe factory. The people phoning me, sometimes three times a day, were men. Once I had this information, I could pass it to the minister and the police." Only at this point, having conducted the investigation himself, did he inform the police. He told the thieves he had their money and arranged to exchange the painting for the cash on August 4, a symbolically chosen date, as it is the Feast of Saint Dominic, founder of Father Zerafa's order.

"We decided to have the operation at my office at the museum. The police had a helicopter and a number of cars going round . . . the government wanted to make this a big show!" But the spectacle nearly ruined the day, as the thieves spotted the helicopter and tried to escape. "The helicopter was following their car, so the police decided to arrest them immediately." But the painting wasn't in the car. Two men were arrested (a third escaped) and finally led the police to the Caravaggio. After the arrest, a policeman told Father Zerafa the thieves had paid an associate £5,000 to kidnap him during the swap. The police hadn't wanted to spook him, but an officer had secretly been assigned as his bodyguard all that day.

Unfortunately, the thieves had an excellent lawyer. "A policeman told them it was no use denying what they'd done, because their phones had been tapped. But they started a constitutional case because the phone tapping used to identify them was totally illegal." The case dragged on for years, during which time both of the arrested thieves died, one of natural causes and one of a drug overdose: "The suspicion is that it was administered to shut him up!" The painting was back, but it had been badly damaged—awkwardly cut from its stretcher, rolled for transport, then mutilated by its kidnappers. Father Zerafa later penned a book about his adventures, the sadly out-of-print *Caravaggio Diaries*. After a career that spanned painting to priesthood at the fore of the Dominican order, with sojourns teaching art history in Rome, studies at Oxford and La Sorbonne, and an eventual rise to become director of Malta's museums, Father Zerafa's outdueling of Caravaggio thieves is still the highlight of a storied career. At eighty-seven he is still going strong, traveling the world to talk about art, even with an active social media presence. When asked about the key to his vivacity, Father Zerafa smiles: "I drink and smoke a lot."

The Met Python's Flying Circus

In the 1970s, a group of friends in town near Rome spent their weekends digging around the ancient Etruscan tombs that dot the Italian countryside around their homes. These *tombaroli*, or tomb raiders, supplemented their income by selling antiquities that they would dig up themselves to local dealers, who would then sell them for hundreds of thousands of dollars. Major museums around the world bought such looted antiquities, including the Metropolitan Museum of Art, the MFA in Boston, and the Getty. The question was, did the museums know that they were buying looted antiquities, or is it simply a case that they should have known but chose to leap at the chance to acquire an ancient masterpiece that seemed too good to be true?

One such object was seized in August 2017 from the Met. It is a vase attributed to the ancient Greek artist Python that a colleague of mine, Cambridge-based Greek archaeologist Christos Tsirogiannis, recognized as having been among the roughly four thousand Polaroids seized when Giacomo Medici, one of the two kingpins of the illicit trade in antiquities looted from Italy (the other protagonist in the field was Gianfranco Becchina), was arrested (their stories have been told many times, for instance, in *The Medici Conspiracy*, *The Lost Chalice*, *Chasing Aphrodite*, *I Predatori dell'Arte Perduta*, and in the *Journal of Art Crime*). Tsirogiannis has made an academic specialization of linking images of looted antiquities (often photographed when police seize goods, or appearing in photographs taken by looters in order to find buyers) to objects that appear on the art market or in major collections.

While Tsirogiannis published his suspicions about the Met Python vase in a 2014 issue of the *Journal of Art Crime*, and sent his findings to the Met, they did nothing about it. This is not uncommon—there are scores of suspect items in major collections, with famous museums sometimes knowingly acquiring looted art (as famously demonstrated in books like the ones mentioned above) and then plotting to cover up their knowledge, in order to play innocent if someone, like Tsirogiannis, calls them on it. The Getty is the most famous such example, but it is not the only one.

Looting of archaeological sites is an international plague that both loses critical historical and archaeological context that could come from supervised excavations of archaeological sites, and it often involves organized crime and, sometimes, terrorist groups which profit from the sale of looted antiquities, thereby fueling and funding all manner of more sinister activities. Of the hundreds of antiquities illegally excavated around the Etruscan necropolis of Cerveteri, just outside of Rome, the two most famous works are some of the only extant creations by the Greek master vase painter Euphronios: a krater, which was bought by the Metropolitan Museum of Art for $1 million, and a kylix, or chalice for wine, which was bought by a Texas billionaire and eventually ended up at the Getty. Both were excavated by the same group of tomb raiders and sold to the same crooked antiques dealer, Giacomo Medici.

The story of that famous chalice is a case in point, and one that has been thoroughly researched. Rarely do we know a complete story of looter-to-famous-collection so clearly (the story is told in *The Lost Chalice*). It began in the early 1970s, where a group of *tombaroli* unearthed Euphronios's chalice and a larger krater from their resting place at the Greppe Sant'Angelo tomb complex in Cerveteri, Italy. The larger krater ended up in the Metropolitan Museum of Art (the famous Euphronios krater), while the smaller chalice was transported through Zürich, where it was eventually purchased by "Bunky" Hunt, a Texas oil tycoon who at one time tried to corner the world's silver market, in anticipation of a Jewish-backed conspiracy to convert the United States to communism. Yes, you read that correctly.

Fast-forward twenty years to a Sotheby's auction, where Hunt's collection was sold in order to avoid bankruptcy and pay off a debt to the Internal Revenue Service. The chalice was purchased by a "European dealer" who was identified as Giacomo Medici, and who was also involved in the sale of the larger krater years before. Having been involved with now two of only nine known pieces by Euphronios, both of which depict the death of Zeus's son Sarpedon, raised too many questions about Giacomo Medici. The Italian Carabinieri began to investigate, along with Manhattan prosecutors. As the investigation unfolded, numerous questions arose about the role of not only the auction house but of the Metropolitan and Getty museums, too.

By the time the smoke cleared, the inquiry had mushroomed well beyond the Euphronios vases, to encompass a literal warehouse in Geneva full of looted, stolen, smuggled, and trafficked antiquities from the Italian countryside. It also implicated a host of major figures from the Metropolitan, the Getty, and other renowned art dealers and galleries. An astounding fifty-two stolen pieces were identified at the Getty and another twenty-two at the Metropolitan—but more have risen to the surface since then, including the Met Python vase. Thus, a questionable provenance or the lack of legitimacy for one small Greek wine cup produced one of the landmark cases in the history of art crime and put the world on notice that the theft and smuggling of art would no longer be tolerated by law enforcement and would not be condoned either directly or even subtly by the major galleries, museums, and auction houses.

There are tens of thousands of artworks reported stolen each year (twenty to thirty thousand per year in Italy alone), and far more that go unreported.

Antiquities taken directly from the earth or the sea fall into the unreported category, as there is no modern record of them.

Authorities might come across a looted tomb, but they cannot know what was in the tomb in the first place, and therefore would not know what to look for. The scale of the illicit trade in antiquities is staggering, made that much more sinister by the frequent involvement of organized crime groups. Looted antiquities can be sold on an open market, for full value, with only a false provenance that suggests that they were legally excavated and exported—but many museums and collectors do not even insist on checking the provenance.

Tsirogiannis has spotted scores of suspicious works, as have colleagues who engage in similar detective work, including Stefano Alessandrini (the right-hand man of Italy's equivalent to the attorney general, who also teaches on the ARCA Program) and David Gill. They regularly inform the institutions in question, assuming that the museums and auction houses and galleries are engaged in best practices, and will take appropriate measures to double-check objects in the collection and turn them in, if they prove indeed to be suspicious. But this recent case shows that best practices are sometimes not adhered to. Frustrated by a lack of response, Tsirogiannis sent his findings to Matthew Bogdanos, at the New York District Attorney's Office. He launched the formal investigation that resulted in the seizure of the Python vase on July 24. With reputations on the line, sometimes millions in purchased antiquities, and even the occasional cover-up to cover up, it often requires police intervention to get collectors, sellers, and collections to do the right thing with objects that appear suspicious. It's a good thing that we have this small, but dedicated, handful of looted art detectives keeping their diligent eyes on art market prizes.

The Myth of the Art Thief

The day after Thanksgiving 1985, 9 a.m., at the University of Arizona Museum of Art. What appeared to be a middle-aged woman and a young man, both in winter overcoats (despite it being fifty-five degrees out), entered the museum, the first visitors of the day. After wandering the galleries for less than ten minutes, the woman asked a guard some questions. Soon after, the two visitors hurried out of the museum. Noting this odd behavior, a guard quickly surveyed the collection and spotted a painting missing, cut from its frame. Willem de Kooning's *Woman-Ochre*, valued then at half a million dollars, now considered worth tens of millions. Sketches were made of the suspects, but the FBI and local police had little else to go on.

That was until 2015, when the estate of a Jerome Alter, who had lived not far from the museum, was evaluated by a local antiques dealer. Among the more interesting items spotted was *Woman-Ochre*, which was hanging in the master bedroom of the Alters' home, visible only when the bedroom door was closed, obscured by it when the door was open. The dealer acquired the painting, not knowing its author or value—he paid just $2,000 for it. It was only years later, when some customers mentioned that the painting, which remained at his shop, looked like a de Kooning, actually like the de Kooning that some folks mentioned had been stolen, that the dealer took action and turned the painting in to the police.

Now investigators are working backward: the artwork has been recovered, but the unlikely suspect, Jerome Alter, died years ago. Some wonder if he and his wife, or even he and his son (if he had dressed in drag, as the female suspect sketch supposedly resembles him), were the ones to have stolen it. Or did they, like the antiques dealer, acquire it from someone else, without knowing that it was hot?

The truth behind art crime is a truth that is misunderstood by the general public and professionals alike—it is far more sinister, and more intriguing. Art crime has its share of cinematic thefts and larger-than-life characters, but it is also the realm of international organized crime syndicates, the involvement of which results in art crime funding all manner of other serious crimes, including the drug trade and terrorism. Art crime has shifted from a relatively innocuous, ideological crime into a major international plague, one of the highest-grossing criminal trades worldwide. But the general public is still stuck in this romanticized image of art thieves as looking and acting like Pierce Brosnan or Cary Grant. Thomas Crown stole art for fun and to admire it, in his cinematic incarnation. But how many real-life art thieves fit this description?

This is the question I'm most likely to be asked when I teach the history of art crime in the summer ARCA Program in Art Crime and Cultural Heritage Protection. The answer is easy: there have been almost no known, real-life art thieves who steal art in order to admire it. But the general public, and the world of criminals, seem to believe that this is the norm. This goes hand in glove with another popular misconception: that there exist criminal collectors who commission the theft of artworks, or regularly buy art that they know was stolen from extant collections. This, too, has happened so infrequently in known history that it is negligible, from a criminological standpoint (compared to the tens of thousands of reported art thefts worldwide, such instances number in the dozens only). But that does not stop the misconception from radically affecting criminal activity. We'll set aside the idea of criminal art collectors for a separate chapter. For now, what about those who steal art from extant collections (meaning that the art's legal location and ownership are known) because, well, they like art and want to keep it at home?

Within this category of thief/collectors, we must divide case studies into subcategories and consider to which, if any, Jerome Alter might belong? There have been some thieves who suffered from kleptomania, a psychological compulsion to steal, and this happened to be focused on art. Stéphane Breitwieser is a Swiss waiter who stole, and kept, at least 239 paintings, worth over a billion dollars, never trying to sell any of them. Sent to prison for this pastime, shortly after he got out, he resumed compulsively stealing art and was back in prison in no time. But Jerome Alter, from what is known of his life story, was no kleptomaniac. There are thieves who stole art for other reasons but wound up keeping it. Adam Worth swiped the world's most expensive painting at the time, 1876, because he planned to ransom it to help spring his brother from custody. But when his brother's lawyer did the job for him, Worth (called "the Napoleon of Crime" and inspiration for Professor Moriarty in the Sherlock Holmes stories) ended up keeping Gainsborough's *Portrait of Georgiana, Duchess of Devonshire* for twenty-five years. Vincenzo Peruggia stole Leonardo's *Mona Lisa* in 1911 ostensibly for ideological reasons—he claimed to have thought it had been looted from his native Italy by Napoleon (a fair guess, but not the case) and thus smuggled it from Paris, where he kept it for two years, to Florence, where he returned it to the Uffizi, and appeared entirely surprised to find himself arrested. These thieves kept the art they stole, but they stole it with a different initial rationale. Perhaps Jerome Alter stole the de Kooning, if indeed he did, with another plan in mind as to how to profit from it, but this also bears no relation to his known biography. Most art is stolen by members of organized crime groups and no one seems to think that Alter was a criminal. Steve Cooperman stole his own paintings, hid them away, and tried to claim their insurance value. But this, likewise, is not the case for Alter. There is no such thing as a professional art thief—this is another Hollywood myth. There are some thieves who have stolen art more than once, and who quite like the cinematic sound of being called an "art thief," but history includes few to none who stole art as their primary criminal activity.

If Alter was the thief, then he joins a miniature group of known, historical thieves who did not steal compulsively, who were not career criminals, and who took a single object, on one occasion, apparently because they liked it and thought it would look nice in their bedroom. The most famous example of such a person, the case that breaks the rule? Pablo Picasso. In 1907, he and an accomplice stole a pair of ancient Iberian statue heads from the Louvre Museum. He kept the heads hidden in his sock drawer, and they appear in his

1907 painting *Les Demoiselles d'Avignon*, the artwork that launched modernism. But aside from Pablo, the historical cupboard of Hollywood-y art thieves is decidedly bare. Maybe we can add one Jerome to the mix? How fitting that his surname is Alter.

Stealing Caravaggio: The Odessa File

On July 31, 2008, a Caravaggio was stolen in the night from a museum in Odessa, Ukraine. The thieves outsmarted an antiquated alarm system by removing a pane of glass from the window, instead of breaking it. Once inside the Museum of Western and Eastern Art, the thieves, almost certainly members of an organized crime syndicate, sliced the canvas off of its stretcher and disappeared into the night, without tripping a single alarm. An original Caravaggio can fetch upward of $50 million at auction. But though the thieves were almost certainly unaware of this fact, the stolen "Caravaggio" is a copy.

To be precise, the Odessa *Taking of Christ* is a contemporary copy of Caravaggio's original *Taking of Christ*, which is in the National Gallery of Dublin. The Odessa copy was proclaimed an original by Soviet historians in the 1950s. But a 1993 article by art historian Sergio Benedetti proved what anyone who is familiar with Caravaggio's work could see from looking at the painting—it was a good, contemporary copy. The figures, particularly that of Christ, are different (and less refined) than Caravaggio's normal work. The easiest comparison is to juxtapose the Dublin and the Odessa pictures. The Dublin picture is lighter, and yet more brooding, and the figures are sharper. While an original Caravaggio could fetch $50–100 million at auction, a contemporary copy will bring in six figures, perhaps low seven. While that's nothing to sneeze at, it is highly unlikely that the thieves knew that they were stealing a copy, worth less than 10 percent of an original Caravaggio.

Caravaggio's technique was revolutionary. No one in Rome had painted with the naturalism he did, particularly in religious works. Caravaggio also popularized a technique called chiaroscuro, the painting of light emerging from darkness, so that figures gradually and dramatically emerge from an amorphous black background. While religious institutions often deemed Caravaggio's work "indecorous" (read as: it didn't look like they expected it to), a passionate group of important private collectors launched Caravaggio's fame in Rome in the first decade of the seventeenth century. Artists had never seen work like Caravaggio's, and they flocked to Rome like pilgrims to learn from him. But Caravaggio was a violent, and thoroughly unpleasant man. He got in a fight with a waiter over an overcooked artichoke, and killed a member of a rival street gang, ostensibly over a game of tennis. Unlike almost every other great artist of his time, he did not have a studio nor did he take on apprentices. In fact, he threatened to kill those who emulated his style. This didn't stop him from being the most frequently copied artist of his time, in both exact reproductions of his paintings and artists appropriating his signature style. The so-called Caravaggisti, among whom the painter of the Odessa *Taking of Christ* no doubt numbered, were a generation younger than Caravaggio, emulating his style and, in some cases, directly copying his works. It is of interest to note that the original Dublin *Taking of Christ* was first believed to have been a copy by one of the Dutch Caravaggisti, Gerrit van Honthorst, before it was correctly attributed to the master himself.

According to police and criminologists, Ukraine is rife with organized crime, with the Balkan Mafia particularly active. Their history of stealing art for trade or collateral in deals for drugs and arms suggests that this latest theft is another that can be attributed to them. They almost certainly, however, do not read art history publications like *Burlington Magazine*, which published the 1993 article proving that the Odessa *Taking of Christ* was a copy.

So, is the last laugh on them? Are the undereducated Mafia undone by their own lack of research? Unfortunately for poetic justice, no. The thieves are not the only ones who may have missed the *Burlington Magazine* article. Most people think that the Odessa painting is an original—especially if they believe most world newspaper articles, which reported that it is an original Caravaggio worth $100 million. It seems that most newspaper reporters did as little research as the thieves. Among other criminals, the thieves can present newspaper clippings "proving" that their stolen Caravaggio is original and simply ignore those who might point out its inauthenticity.

Though *The Taking of Christ* has since been recovered, the coda to the story of the Odessa "Caravaggio" remains mysterious. Police never disclosed to the public either the nature of the recovery of the painting, nor the identity of the thieves. Police only reported that the organizer of the crime had been murdered, leading to speculation on whom it might have been.

On December 6, 2008, the Ukrainian newspaper *Weekly Mirror* reported: "According to information received by *WM* (*Weekly Mirror*) from sources close to the Ministry of the Interior, state law-enforcement agencies have recovered the Caravaggio painting *The Taking of Christ, or the Kiss of Judas*. The painting was stolen from the Odessa Museum of Western and Eastern Art in July of last year. . . . According to several sources, the organizer of the theft, who has been under investigation for several months, was found dead."

Three days later, on December 9, 2008, another article linked the death of the organizer to the recovery of the painting: "According to unconfirmed information, the organizer of the theft was found murdered several months ago." This statement would place the murder of the organizer of the theft soon after the July 31 theft itself.

Or does another murder, one which corresponds to the recovery of the stolen painting, shed more direct light on the organizer of the crime? The question of the identity of the murdered crime organizer remains undisclosed by police. But Nikolai Ponomarenko is a strong possible candidate.

The murder of Ponomarenko, a wealthy Ukrainian art collector, was reported in the *Economic News* on December 8, 2008: "Viktor Razvadovskii, the chief of police for the Kharkov region, has announced that a valuable painting has been found in the home of the murdered art collector Nikolai Ponomarenko, but that this painting 'is not a Caravaggio,' the Ukrainian newspaper *Today* reported." The find has been sent off for an examination of its authenticity and value. The subject of the painting, which depicts sheep, has nothing in common with the subject of the stolen masterpiece. Nevertheless, Ukrainian law enforcement officials report that they are close to solving the Caravaggio affair.

According to Vasilii Presnyazhnuk, prosecutor for the Odessa region, authorities in one region of Ukraine have seized an automobile transporting five original paintings valued at "three million euros or more." The tone of the police statement, declaring emphatically that the stolen painting found at Ponomarenko's home "is not a Caravaggio" and that it in fact "depicts sheep," sounds a bit as though the lady doth protest too much. If the police were feeling coy, and if one were to credit them with more art historical acumen than reality likely warrants, one might say that the stolen painting found at Ponomarenko's home indeed "is not a Caravaggio"—because neither was *The Taking of Christ* stolen from the museum.

Whether or not the painting found at Ponomarenko's home was *The Taking of Christ*, the fact of stolen art having been found at the home of a murdered art collector is certainly telling. It is perhaps a giveaway that the journalist has allowed the murder of Ponomarenko to segue into a statement that the Caravaggio affair was near its end. The recovery of the "Caravaggio" was announced the very next day, on December 9, leading to the logical conclusion that the aforementioned Ponomarenko affair and the car full of stolen art led directly to the recovery of *The Taking of Christ*.

On a few matters, the available facts seem to agree. Organized crime was behind the theft of *The Taking of Christ*. Ponomarenko's murder was linked to stolen art. The organizer of the theft, perhaps Ponomarenko himself but certainly someone linked to him, was murdered following the theft. Ponomarenko was involved in the illicit art trade, as a buyer if not an organizer. No one in authority wished to disclose further details about the recovery of the stolen painting, which further arouses suspicion that the recovery is part of a multifaceted move against a crime syndicate, the revelation of which would derail the larger investigation.

Russian and Ukrainian organized crime experts made several statements to the media regarding art crime in Ukraine that diverge from the general understanding elsewhere in the world. While it is agreed upon that crimes such as the Odessa theft are most often perpetrated by organized crime groups, the destination of the works stolen in Ukraine is, according to these authorities, criminal collectors: "In the nineties the antiques Mafia worked to export. Now they steal for themselves," asserts the head of the department of local investigation of the Ministry of Internal Affairs of Ukraine, Vladimira Gusak. "Basically, rare pieces find their way into the private collections of well-to-do Ukrainians."

In reality, very few individuals who could be categorized as "criminal collectors" have played a role in known art crimes over the past fifty years. The presence of criminal collectors is a popular misconception. Identifiable works of fine art stolen from public collections, such as *The Taking of Christ*, are much more likely to be held for ransom, or traded on a closed black market between criminal groups. Despite this, unnamed "specialists" suggest that private collectors are responsible for the majority of fine art thefts in Russia and Ukraine: "Black market 'specialists' assert that oligarch-Mafia men have paid at least $100 million for the painting and are hiding it from the public gaze in their apartments. Their professional colleagues at the museum suggest that in this case we are dealing with a premeditated, commissioned crime. . . . So, it is most likely that the treasure is sitting in the private collection of some sort of oligarch whom the detectives will never reach."

Such a statement could mean that art crime functions differently in Russia and Ukraine than the rest of the world or could mean that the "specialists" interviewed about this case share the same popular misconceptions as much of the rest of the world. The mention of certainty that "oligarch-Mafia men have paid at least $100 million for the painting" tells us that the thieves were able to convince at least someone that *The Taking of Christ* is by Caravaggio, when the rest of the art history world knows that it is not. Were there any question of the painting's value, the thieves need only have brandished any of the international newspaper articles that blazed headlines "$100 Million Caravaggio Stolen from Odessa" to provide their proof of its value. World newspapers wouldn't lie, would they? Probably not, at least not intentionally. But they would allow their enthusiasm for a hot story to impair the diligence of their research, effectively handing organized crime $100 million, when the actual value of the stolen painting was likely less than 1 percent of that figure.

Theft as Art, Art as Theft

The heist went down like this.

A very ugly, highly suspicious iron-red van pulled up opposite the New National Gallery in Berlin and was left running. Out of it walked a tall, slender man in a *Kleppermantel*, a graphite-colored raincoat, and on into the museum. After leaving this at the coat check, he walked down to the basement, with a pair of wire-cutter pliers in his pocket. He passed through a climate-control glass barrier until he stood before three small Romantic German paintings by Carl Spitzweg, including one that was an icon to all mid-twentieth-century Germans—*The Poor Poet*. But there was a guard, too close for comfort, and the slender man had to get rid of him. On the wall opposite *The Poor Poet* was a painting of chess players, so he turned to stand before it, and he started laughing, loudly, almost maniacally. The guard approached him, looked at the painting, and asked, "What's so funny?" Heart thundering, the slender man spun and dashed to *The Poor Poet*, clipped the wire on which it hung with his pliers, ripped it off the wall, and ran. He passed through the climate barrier as the alarm blared. He flew up the stairs, through the foyer, wove around the crowd of people clogging the entrance as they waited to get in, crashed through the emergency exit, the painting under his arm, and sprinted to the car. Adrenaline pumping, the guards close behind, he slipped on the snow outside, as a guard screamed, "Now we get him!" But he was up on his feet and kept running to the very ugly, highly suspicious van. He had locked all the doors but propped the lock to the driver's door open with chewing gum. Now he pulled it open, jumped inside, slammed and locked it behind him, as the guards tore at the handle. A guard was holding the handle of the door as he lurched the van forward.

The slender man was off.

If this sounds like the opening of a movie, perhaps it should be. It is actually a firsthand account by the famous conceptual artist Ulay of what he calls "the Berlin lifting," formally entitled *Irritation: There's a Criminal Touch to Art*, his 1976 theft-as-performance.

Frank Uwe Laysiepen, known as Ulay, was in Berlin because his partner in life and art at the time, Marina Abramović, was engaged in a solo work there. In anticipation of her performance, Ulay visited the New National Gallery. On a wall, a small painting that resonated with every German of his age: Carl Spitzweg's *The Poor Poet*, painted in 1839.

Now, this is not a painting that non-Germans would be likely to know, as it owes its fame to the dubious distinction of having been one of Hitler's favorites. It shows, in a slight caricature of naturalism, an aged poet, in once-fine, now-tattered clothes, lying in bed under a torn blanket, his quill pen in his mouth. His tiny garret apartment employs a pocked umbrella to plug a leak against the rain. He is composing a poem, conducting the rhythm of the verse with curled fingers, while books line the mattress on the floor that is his only piece of furniture. But it is so cold that he is feeding any paper he can find into his small, tiled stove—including the precious poems he is so carefully writing, and for which he lives. It is a painting of charm and irony, à la O. Henry's 1905 story, "The Gift of the Magi": the poet must destroy what he lives for in order to continue to live. Ulay recalled this as the only color reproduction in a book he was given in grade school. The Hitler connection carried the tiny painting, just about the right size to fit under one's arm, to prominence and made it a loaded object in postwar Germany.

Interested in doing a performance in Berlin, Ulay had the idea to place Berlin's high-end art institutions in stark contrast to the neighborhood of Kreuzberg, where he found a large Turkish immigrant community, which he describes as "completely run down, shabby, ugly, a terrible ghetto-like place." The plan was to weave together German high art, marginalized immigrants, and this painting—a symbol of both German high art and the nation's regrettable recent history, which Ulay would call his "trigger."

He began "casing the joint," what criminologists refer to as "hostile surveillance." He spent a week planning, always with performance in mind—as he says, "I wanted to do everything with my hands and feet, not with high-tech equipment." The paintings were wired—removing them from the wall would sound an alarm. The main entrance was via revolving doors that would automatically lock shut if the alarm went off. But the requirements of fire safety ran broadside to museum security. "On either side of the two revolving doors are emergency exits, and they can't be locked. They're sealed by the fire brigade. So I thought, well, to break the seal off the emergency exit and push that door open, and that would be my escape."

He wanted the performance to be documented. Abramović was planted in the New National Gallery before he entered, with Ulay's Super 8 camera, to shoot from inside as the event unfolded. He plotted with his gallerist, Mike Steiner, who assured him that he would cover any legal fees Ulay might incur, should he be arrested either during the performance or afterward. He had a very hard time finding anyone willing to film what was, quite literally, a crime, but he eventually settled on Jörg Schmidt-Reitwein, who was a fine cameraman (he'd worked with Werner Herzog) but was only willing to follow the event in a separate car, and refused to get out of the car, in order to keep a thin wall of automotive steel insulating him from the crime itself.

On Saturday, December 11, 1976, Ulay wrote up a concept of the performance, which he calls "the action": a recipe in fourteen stages for what he planned to do, and a diagram outlining it, "like a little pyramid, one institute, the other institute, the third institute, that was a triangle, and then from there I escaped outside, into secularized society." He posted this to the media, knowing that it would not arrive until Monday. He also photographed the Spitzweg and had it blown up on a linen sheet, so that it spanned two meters by one and a half meters, like a billboard. The morning of the theft, a Sunday, he drove to the Academy of Fine Arts, closed for the day, and hung the reproduction of the Spitzweg over the doorway, so that, unfurled, it would entirely block the entrance to this parallel German high art institution to the New National Gallery, where the crime would take place. His escape car was an "incredibly ugly van from the French police, typical of the '68 Paris Revolution, painted matte red, like coagulated iron." There was concern about domestic terrorism in Germany at the time, and this van was as suspicious-looking as he could find. But the van was as unreliable as it was ugly—Sunday morning, he tried starting it unsuccessfully, and he had to push it in second gear to get it going.

Not the ideal getaway vehicle.

Sweating and racing from the New National Gallery, the freshly stolen painting riding shotgun, Ulay drove toward Kreuzberg. He was more worried about cab drivers than the police. "I knew that taxi drivers enjoyed listening to the police radio, for fun. I knew that they would also block roads to help the police, in this time of terrorism." He had intentionally chosen a wildly obvious getaway vehicle, for artistic and symbolic reasons, but this made it very difficult to hide.

He made it to the Kreuzberg district, parked the car, and grabbed the painting. He'd brought a nylon bag with him, in which he would stash the painting, but it wouldn't fit. "The painting was bigger than I thought. Not big, but with this baroque frame, it was very heavy." So he had to carry it under his arm. He ran past a poster of a Berlin gallery exhibition. Out of the nylon bag he pulled a small color reproduction of the Spitzweg, which he pinned over the poster, before thundering on down the street.

"I had been visiting several Turkish families," he says, "but one was willing to collaborate. I didn't say anything about the stolen painting, I said we were making a documentary film and was it possible to use their ambiance, just to hang the painting briefly, while we film." Though Schmidt-Reitwein hadn't wanted to get out of the car to film, in the heat of the moment he followed Ulay, the camera bouncing on his shoulder.

Before Ulay went into the family's apartment, he stopped at a phone booth on the street and did something that a criminal would find, well, unexpected. "I called the museum, because I wanted to talk to Professor Dieter Honisch, who was director at the time. I wanted to say, 'Listen I have stolen the painting. I want you to come and just testify that I have not damaged or destroyed it, that's all. And I take all the consequences.'" But the police had already been called in and were manning the phones. So Ulay explained where he was to the police and said they should come retrieve the painting. Then he went inside. "I rushed up to the second floor, rang the bell, they opened the door, the lady with a couple of children around her. I went in there, I didn't carry a hammer or nails, so I took one of their paintings off the wall and hung the Spitzweg in its place."

There was an interminable wait for the police to arrive. "I was completely freaked out," Ulay recalls. "It was cold, I smoked one cigarette after the other, it was snowing, it was so miserable and I was waiting for the consequences." He hoped that he would not be sent to prison, that his action would be recognized as a political statement, not something genuinely threatening, but the state was unlikely to have much of a sense of humor about such things. In some twenty minutes, the police arrived, sealing off the block. After all, they didn't know if this call was a prank, a trap, or something even less expected—a performance artist turning himself in. After some time, two men came, a driver in civilian clothes and Professor Honisch. Honisch introduced himself and said that the other man was his assistant but soon after whispered to Ulay that the "assistant" was, in fact, a police officer. It seemed that Honisch was sympathetic.

Honisch confirmed that the painting was unharmed, and Ulay said that he was prepared to take responsibility for his action. He was driven back to the New National Gallery and was seated in Honisch's office there. "I made a statement that this was a demonstrative action, not a theft in the traditional sense." Ulay does not refer to it as a performance but considers it a "protest action, first of all against the institutionalization of art, secondarily about discrimination against foreign workers." That was all well and good, but he was put in jail overnight, before the civil hearing. He had one phone call, so he rang Mike Steiner, his gallerist, who had promised to sort out a lawyer. Steiner was popping the champagne, considering this action a great success, while Ulay spent the night in lockdown.

The next morning, he was brought before a judge, and the prosecutor read out a list of crimes. Ulay recalls, "Man, I saw myself in prison for a really long time." He had hoped that it would all be dismissed. But the judge seemed considerate. "The judge was young, cool, quiet, and when the prosecutor finished reading the list of transgressions, the judge asked me to give my own interpretation of the event." Ulay was about to start and just about got out the words "demonstrative action," when the door to the courtroom burst open and in walks the lawyer Mike Steiner sorted out for him. "Somebody came in, I didn't know who, and shouted a name, I think Ernst, and the judge went, 'Karl'! So obviously they were old friends. And that was my lawyer." Mike had chosen precisely the right man for the job. Whether it was the lawyer friend or an innate sympathy for Ulay's version of the story, the judge sided with him and against the prosecutor, and was inclined toward leniency. Ulay's citizenship complicated matters. Born in Germany, he was at the time a Dutch citizen, living in Amsterdam. There would have to be a proper trial in three months' time. The prosecutor was concerned that Ulay would head back to the Netherlands and not return for the trial. Turned out he was right. "Three months later, there was a trial at the court in Berlin. I didn't go," says Ulay. "Neither did anybody else. I was given, I think, thirty-six days' imprisonment or a buyout of 3,600 deutsch marks. I never had so much money." But it was a moot point, as he'd skipped the trial.

The Spitzweg went back to its place in the New National Gallery.

He'd gotten away with it.

Well, almost.

The sixteen-millimeter film was saved, a documentary-style vision of the event recorded from the second car by Schmidt-Reitwein. And Abramović had managed to run one roll of film, then pop it out of the camera, espionage style, concealing it from the police. Ulay explains, "I had positioned her [in the gallery basement] and explained the camera, because she never made film before. She couldn't see very well. But the roll of film is three minutes, and can shoot eighteen images per second. She ran through it, to the end, took the film out, inserted the new roll, and put the finished roll in her boots or her bra or something, as I'd prepped her to do. Because I know that, if the police come and see people with a camera, they'd confiscate it." This spy-like trick meant that the police seized an unexposed, empty roll of film from Abramović, and her perspective inside the museum could be edited with the film shot by Schmidt-Reitwein.

One year later, Ulay and Abramović were visiting a wealthy collector friend in Wiesbaden, Michael Berger. "Wiesbaden was so miserable, the roads were frozen, everything was ice, we were miserable, poor, still living in our van. And we said, 'We need some sun.'" Berger generously agreed to buy them tickets to anywhere they liked, for a holiday. They chose Morocco, and he booked them a flight from Frankfurt. Unfortunately, this route required a stopover in Munich that, for whatever reason, went through customs. "And there they caught me," Ulay sighs. "I was standing there, they just had a black book with the bad guys listed in it, and they caught me and arrested me. Thirty-six days' imprisonment or 3,600 deutsch marks." This was a nasty surprise, although one that might have been predictable. "I thought I got away with it," explains Ulay. "So I called Michael Berger from Munich and said, 'Michael, I got a big problem you know, I got arrested again . . .'" Berger sent his brother, who lived in Munich, to bail Ulay out. He was free for the moment. He skipped bail. No Morocco. And he still had not served his time.

But this wasn't quite the end of the story. Back in Amsterdam, Ulay was summoned to speak with the German consul. He tried to explain that he was a poor artist who couldn't afford the 3,600 deutsch marks, but the consul said, "That's no good, you know, sooner or later, they will get you. And he was right." Ulay eventually crossed the Dutch-German border, hoping for the best, and he was taken off the train and arrested. "They put me in a terrorist prison. Unbelievable. And I was there, convicted as a social delinquent, for ten or fourteen days. But I had great meditation time, and it was probably the period in which I read the most books in my life."

So, the crime, or rather the demonstrative action, was punished to a certain degree, but the "Berlin lifting" event lived on and has become one of the best-known, and most admired, works of performance art in history. Even if Ulay doesn't like to call it a performance.

Why Do People Attack Art?

On Saturday, March 18, 2017, a man "with no fixed abode" slashed Thomas Gainsborough's *The Morning Walk* (1785) with a screwdriver, at London's National Gallery. He was quickly detained by visitors and museum staff, and the damage appears to be fixable—the paint was cut, but the screwdriver did not pierce all the way through the supporting canvas. Conservators are brilliant surgeons and the scars should be invisible by the time they are done and *The Morning Walk* is back on the wall. If you need evidence of this, just stroll to a nearby room at the same museum and look at Velazquez's *Rokeby Venus*. It was knifed in 1914 by a suffragette who was outraged at the arrest of Emmeline Pankhurst for her protestation in favor of women's right to vote. These slash marks were carefully healed and only three pale, barely visible scars can be seen on Venus's back. A similarly impressive repair can (barely) be spotted on Rubens's *Adoration of the Magi* at King's College Chapel, Cambridge. In 1974, an IRA activist carved the letters "I-R-A" into the canvas. The patching was so good that, today, the ghosts of those letters can only be seen when you examine the work at a sharp angle and against slanting light.

But these attacks prompt questions. First, could security at major museums like the National Gallery be improved, to prevent such incidents, however infrequent they may be? Second, why on earth would anyone decide to attack a work of art, particularly one as innocuous and unobjectionable as a Gainsborough portrait? And third, is the way that we in the media handle attacks on art just compounding the problem?

Having worked with numerous security directors of major museums, I know that there is a balance to strike between keeping art safe and fulfilling the museum's purpose of making it accessible to the public. There is no such thing as a risk-free museum, but there is a way to minimize risk of damage and theft, a way that many top museums have chosen (the Louvre, the Prado, the Van Gogh, the Uffizi, to name a few), but which the National Gallery has not. That is to install airport-style security at the entrance. It is a modest inconvenience to museumgoers, but one that they will be used to, from travel in this day and age: moving single-file through a metal detector, bags scanned, before entering the museum to explore freely. This method would prevent attacks with metal objects, like knives and screwdrivers, and would be a strong deterrent to any attacks at all—potential perpetrators are likely to be scared off by having to pass under the scrutiny of security and move slowly into the museum, clearly filmed on CCTV, and with nervous or suspicious behavior likely to be noted before they even enter. In an era of concern over terrorist attacks on populous sites, this is also a good idea. Of course, a determined baddie can still find ways to damage art, but the risk is mitigated. Such security is also the best deterrent for thieves, who would have to enter and exit via a gauntlet of security and a tangle of guests.

Why certain art is targeted by vandals is a complicated question, and the attack on a seemingly unobjectionable portrait of an eighteenth-century couple is, frankly, bizarre and suggests that there may have been no motive linked to the content of the painting itself (we'll get to that in a moment). I ask my ARCA students to chart characteristics of art in danger of being attacked, and it falls into specific categories, if we look back at dozens of historical examples of vandalism, from *Mona Lisa* to *Guernica* to Michelangelo's *David* and *Pieta*, to *The Night Watch*, and so on. Such acts that have an ideological rationale for the object targeted represent one category: the destruction of Catholic statuary during the Reformation, the Taliban's dynamiting the Bamiyan Buddhas, ISIS's smashing of ancient sculptures, and even American soldiers tearing down statues of Saddam Hussein during the Iraq conflict. People strike out at objects that symbolize an idea that they wish to damage, with the artworks acting as a stand-in. Vandalism is the random defacing of objects, in which there might be a message that the attacker wishes to send, but their choice of target is not a loaded one.

Art that tends to be targeted usually falls into one of three categories. It may be very famous, and attacking it is seen as a good way to get attention, like John Hinckley trying to murder then-president Ronald Reagan in order to get actress Jodie Foster to notice him. It may be religiously or politically charged, like Chris Ofili's *The Virgin Mary* (made with elephant dung) or Andres Serrano's *Immersion (Piss Christ)*. Or it might be sexually provocative, like my favorite painting, Bronzino's *Allegory of Love and Lust*. This work, also in London's National Gallery, was attacked in 2003 (the year I was visiting it regularly, writing my master's thesis on it). An unemployed thirty-six-year-old punched the painting once before being tackled by security, doing no damage but prompting the painting to be covered in protective glass. This was not reported in the news at the time. I just happened to notice the glass suddenly installed, as I was visiting the painting several times a week. Artworks that fit these categories are at highest risk. Thomas Gainsborough's *The Morning Walk* fits none of them.

So why was it attacked? Sometimes the rationale offered by vandals has a logic to it, at other times it seems that the art is just a magnet for mental instability. There is a serial Rothko vandal, a known quantity among security directors, who travels around trying to damage paintings by this artist, works so abstract that it's hard to imagine what the objection could be. The suffragette who slashed the *Rokeby Venus* chose to target a work that she felt objectified women, but her main goal was to be interviewed by the press in order to get a public voice to speak out about her cause. The Hungarian man who attacked Michelangelo's *Pieta* with a hammer in 1972 did so while shouting, "I am Jesus Christ, risen from the grave!" The Italian man who, in 1991, attacked Michelangelo's *David* (also with a hammer) rationalized his action by explaining that a painting by Veronese told him to do it (he also recently attacked a plaque in Florence, so he seems to have an enduring mania for this sort of behavior). Let no one doubt that art provokes, stirs emotions, raises passions. Attacking it is also inevitably noteworthy, because art is of extremely high value (financially and culturally), and it is almost certain to be reported in the media.

And now we come to the third point. You may have noticed that I have been careful not to include the names of any vandals in this essay. That is on purpose and is something I would recommend as a policy for all media. We cannot prevent art from moving people, very occasionally even moving them to violence against it. But we can eliminate a frequent rationale for attacking art—achieving one's fifteen minutes of fame. Would Hinckley have attempted to murder Reagan if he had been certain that his name and picture would never be "promoted" by the media (and therefore Jodie Foster would never have known of him)? Would the suffragette have attacked the *Rokeby Venus* had she known that she would not be given a platform to speak about her noble cause to the media? A Veronese painting might still have told someone to whack David's toe with a hammer. But if the media removed the incentive of simply getting attention, by refusing to publish names or photographs of vandals, or their subsequent statements, then it would eliminate one of the motivations for such incidents. Combine that with more universal airport-style security at museum entrances, and we would see significantly fewer thefts and attacks on art.

5 WAR, CONFLICT, AND ART

The Prince and the Statue Thieves: Antiquities and Terrorism in Cambodia

The feet were all wrong. To be precise, they were missing altogether. Just bone-colored stubs, but that in itself was not reason for suspicion. It was the way the stubs ended. Not torn, not broken, but cleanly cut, as if by a modern machine, like a bandsaw.

It was the summer of 2012, and Prince Ravivaddhana Monipong Sisowath, known to his friends as Ravi, was staring at the cover of the Sotheby's catalogue. "My first reaction was, 'once again, Sotheby's,'" he recalls, followed by "this will be a hard recovery to make, because it is basically a problem of money and politics." The footless statue was the star of the sale, estimated at around $2 million, yet it was obviously stolen, looted from a temple in his native Cambodia, the country from which his family, the royal family, had been exiled since 1970, and in which he had first set foot in 2000, age twenty-nine. "I wondered, how can you give a price to something so precious that to me it cannot have a price? I was totally shocked." He picked up the phone and made some calls. Within minutes he knew exactly which temple the life-size statue had been looted from. He knew, because its feet were still there.

The statue in question is called the *Duryodhana*, and it depicts the protagonist of a Sanskrit Hindu epic (thought to have been penned in the ninth century BC), the *Mahabharata*. Duryodhana was the eldest of one hundred sons of a blind king but was muscled out of place as rightful heir when his cousins, the Pandava brothers, led by Bhima, claimed the throne instead. The life-size statue was sculpted around the tenth century, during the height of the Khmer empire. It had been consigned to Sotheby's in 2011 by a Belgian collector, but experts suspect that it had been looted sometime in the 1970s.

Prince Ravi shook his head and sighed. This was but the most recent, and highest-profile, example of a trend that has lasted decades, with its origins in the systematic looting of Cambodian religious sites by the Khmer Rouge, the Communist regime that seized power on March 18, 1970, and prompted the exile of the royal family, a year before Ravi was born. Ravi recalls the first object that drew his attention to the fruits of rampant looting in his homeland. "When I first arrived in Rome, in 1997, there is a shop next to Palazzo Farnese. I went into it because I thought I might be able to afford to buy what I thought was a copy of a Cambodian statue in the window. Then the man named a price which was absolutely incredible. I said, 'Do you mean that this piece is authentic?' He said, 'Yes.' I said, 'Then you are a thief.'" Throughout the Cambodian Civil War (1970–1998) trafficking in looted antiquities, largely taken from temple complexes, was commonplace. There is no estimate as to the number of works stolen, damaged, or destroyed, but visitors today, without venturing off the beaten path, can see hundreds of empty plinths and niches that once housed artworks. It would be a rare and unusual thing to find an authentic Cambodian temple statue on the market that was not stolen. Six major statues, which Ravi refers to as "blood antiques," have been returned to Cambodia from the United States alone: from the Metropolitan Museum of Art in 2023, Sotheby's, Christie's, the Norton Simon Museum, and a sculpture of Hanuman, the monkey god, which was looted from the Prasat Chen temple at Koh Ker in the 1970s, bought by the Cleveland Museum in 1982. Dr. Simon MacKenzie, a criminologist who studies looting in Cambodia as part of the Trafficking Culture research group, based at the Scottish Centre for Crime and Justice Research at University of Glasgow, explains: "Many temple sites we visited were empty shells—still magnificent, of course, but hollowed out by the theft of the statuary. There is a great sadness which comes with visiting these sites, which while still great have been so severely diminished. Everywhere you turn there are plinths with just the feet of a former statue remaining, or statues without heads." It was back in the 1970s that the *Duryodhana* was stolen, cut off at the feet to facilitate transport, and smuggled into Thailand and then abroad, for sale in Europe. Most of the looting during the time of the Khmer Rouge was organized by that regime and therefore funded their activities, which ranged from terrorism to genocide. Unfortunately, remnants of the trafficking networks of the Khmer Rouge era remain in place to this day.

Prince Ravi was not the only one to have noted the cover of the Sotheby's catalogue. The Cambodian government formally requested the removal of the statue from the sale on the morning it was to be auctioned. Sotheby's removed the statue from the sale but refused to hand it over to the Cambodian government, considering it to be the property of the woman who consigned it. Like all auction houses, Sotheby's is a middleman. It sells for a commission but does not buy works directly, so it is not unreasonable that it should refuse to hand over an object on consignment. However, insult was added to injury when a Sotheby's representative suggested that the Cambodian government buy the looted statue from the seller.

Ravi, the great-grandson of King Sisowath Monivong and one of a bevy of Cambodian princes and princesses, wears the soft face of a beautiful youth, a lively smile, and the silky movements of a trained dancer. All members of the royal family train in traditional Cambodian dance from an early age, and Ravi is no exception. He is also a fortune teller, adept at reading cards and charts. At age fourteen, he was uninspired in his piano lessons, and his tutor offered to teach him astrology instead. Rather than disapproving, his mother encouraged the practice, for she too was an astrologer—the royal lineage has practiced such occult arts for millennia. "In my family," Ravi explains, "especially in the Sisowath branch, many princes and princesses are gifted with astrology. My mother, Princess Norodom Daravadey, inherited her talents from her grandmother, Princess Sisowath Bophasy, who was also a great dancer at the time of King Sisowath. And I was taught by my mother." He grew up in Paris and Rome, in a small family, with Chinese servants and an atmosphere of Cambodia rather than France, but otherwise of middle-class character. He is quick to note that no member of the royal family receives handouts or tax money: "Everybody knows in the family that, apart from the king and a very little number of family members who are civil servants, the rest of the family should have a job of his or her own. Earning one's money is absolutely normal for any member of the royal family." They may have blue blood and elite manners, but they work for a living. Ravi works in Rome and uses his extensive Rolodex as a high-end consultant to those who wish to do business in Cambodia and need help with the right connections.

Ravi is the most outspoken and dedicated member of the royal family when it comes to the looting of Cambodian temples, like the Prasat Chen temple at Koh Ker, the source of the *Duryodhana* and the Hanuman monkey god statue. He also served as a program officer for the World Food Programme of the United Nations, and in this capacity he first visited Cambodia, in 2000. While he is more figurehead than foot soldier in the prevention and recovery of looted antiquities, he does what he can to assist the few willing to go into the field, who encounter organized criminals and even terrorists. People like Simon MacKenzie.

Dr. MacKenzie's Trafficking Culture team consists of five researchers and five doctoral students. Funded by the European Research Council, they collect evidence of global looting of cultural objects by conducting regional case studies of trafficking routes. For his research into this field, MacKenzie won the 2014 Eleanor and Anthony Vallombroso Award for Art Crime Scholarship, given annually by ARCA. He and one of his colleagues, Tess Davis, traveled to Cambodia to visit looted sites and do what they could to track down those responsible. What they found was frightening in scale, organization, and physical menace.

MacKenzie and Davis's work was published in the *British Journal of Criminology*, in an article entitled "Temple Looting in Cambodia: Anatomy of a Statue Trafficking Network," and it was republished in *Art Crime: Terrorists, Tomb Raiders, Forgers and Thieves* (a book of academic essays that I edited). In the summer of 2013, MacKenzie and Davis traveled some 2,500 kilometers throughout Cambodia and Thailand to track the route of looted statues from major temple sites, like Koh Ker, and find out who was behind what was once a highly organized, large-scale looting scheme—and which remains remarkably intact to this day. "We have established a picture of a funneling network that moved statues from various temples in Cambodia and passed them into a small network of channels that moved them by oxcart, truck and even elephant out of the country and into Thailand," wrote MacKenzie in a recent article in the *British Journal of Criminology*. Cambodian sites in the northwest of the country, including Koh Ker and Angkor, saw looted objects funneled through Sisophon, a town twenty kilometers from the Cambodian/Thai border. MacKenzie and Davis tracked the trafficking route, through scores of interviews with locals and regularly aware that they were in danger by asking such questions, from Sisophon to Poipet, which straddles the border, and on to Aranyaprathet and Sa Kaeo, in Thailand. From there works were taken to Bangkok and then sold abroad. MacKenzie was able to identify specific criminal networks, routes taken by looters, and even individuals responsible for the looting. "Organized criminals with no military affiliations were active in the looting of Cambodia," he writes. The illicit trade in antiquities went hand in hand with the drug and arms trades, and murders were committed to solidify claims on looting sites and smuggled routes. It has been alleged that the looting of the Koh Ker site may have been done through the personal intervention of Ta Mok, one of the most notorious of the Khmer Rouge masterminds of genocide, who was nicknamed The Butcher. But while there was a historical component to this research, the worrisome fact is that it is still going on. While interviewing locals during his research trip, a looter in Thailand offered Dr. MacKenzie any Cambodian antiquity he might like from a temple, if he would bring a photograph of it.

In 2013, a lawsuit was filed by the Manhattan US Attorney's Office for the return to Cambodia of the *Duryodhana*. "The US wanted to show their good will [toward Cambodia]," Ravi notes, "and so it all went the way it should." The consignor was forced to return the statue with no compensation, but she was not penalized, as there was no evidence brought forth that she knew that the statue was looted when she acquired it. Sotheby's was likewise not penalized, aside from yet another round of negative publicity due to suspect behavior on the part of the individuals in the auction house. They did offer to pay for the shipping of the statue back to Cambodia—no small feat, as it weighs in at half a ton.

The six "blood antiques" returned to Cambodia from US collections represent the tip of the iceberg, but they are a start. In addition to the *Duryodhana*, a pair of comparable statues was voluntarily returned by the Metropolitan Museum of Art, probably taken from the same temple complex, referred to as the *Kneeling Attendants* but that actually represents two of the Pandava brothers, the rival claimants to the throne in the epic *Mahabharata*. In May 2014, yet another statue from the complex, the *Bhima*, was returned from the Norton Simon Museum, where it had been a star of the collection since it was bought from a New York dealer in 1976. It had been looted from the same temple as had the *Duryodhana*. *Bhima*'s feet, still on site at Prasat Chen, were identified in 2006 by archaeologist Eric Bourdonneau, who produced a digital image that matched the feet in Cambodia to the rest of the statue in the United States. By April 2012, a month after the *Duryodhana* was featured on the cover of Sotheby's catalogue, archaeologists in Cambodia further excavated Prasat Chen and found nine pedestals, all of which had once contained statues from this same group—four of which would shortly be restored. The return of the Hanuman monkey god statue from Cleveland, in May 2015, was another victory but, as Ravi pines, "we are still waiting for more sculptures from the Denver Museum of Art and the Met."

The statues returned were displayed together in May 2014 in a special gallery in Cambodia, unveiled in an elaborate ceremony that featured classical dancers whose performance thrilled Ravi. "The return of genuine Khmer artifacts to their homeland was a blessing, thanks to the multilateral efforts to have looted artifacts back in their countries of origin," Ravi said. Hanuman, the monkey god, was recently installed beside them. But as for the personal, spiritual meaning of the return of the statues? "Words are not powerful enough to express my feelings."

It was particularly fitting that the *Bhima*, the *Kneeling Attendants*, the *Duryodhana*, and now the *Hanuman* should have been looted and returned together. In the epic *Mahabharata*, Duryodhana does battle with Bhima and his five Pandava brothers, challengers as heir to the throne, while Hanuman, Bhima's brother, also plays a key role. Their millennia-old battle was mirrored in a traditional Cambodian dance to honor a guest or a spirit when they return to their homeland. The dancers swirled and glided barefoot before the embattled stone warriors, whose feet, sawn-off at the ankles, will never again touch the ground, but who now float above the earth of the nation from which they were ripped decades ago.

The Washington Principles Have Been a Failure

"The Washington Principles have been a failure, and the conference is an attempt to whitewash this failure." So says Marc Masurovsky, and he should know. Masurovsky is one of three cofounders of HARP (Holocaust Art Research Project), which was established in 1997, one year before the Washington Principles were pronounced. Approaching their twentieth anniversary, a planned conference looks set to feature much patting on the shoulders and self-congratulations among the people who formulated what was meant to be a series of guidelines dealing with the restitution of cultural heritage property that had changed hands during the Nazi period, from 1933 until the end of the Second World War. The problem is that, according to Masurovsky and about a dozen other specialists from around the world in this field whose opinions I gathered for this essay, the Washington Principles look and sound good but have been almost completely ineffectual.

Provenance research is a very sticky wicket, and Masurovsky describes it as "a toxic field of study." The issue becomes problematic when research into an artwork's history overturns stones that cover dark recesses of a nation's past. The simple research into an object's "biography" then becomes a political issue, for instance, with Switzerland's resistance to repatriating compelling claims by Jewish families whose art was seized during the Second World War (though one could replace Switzerland with just about any European country, and one can find examples of resistance to what appear to be objectively just claims for the return of looted art). This can make provenance research a matter of individual scholars or families pitted against nations which would rather not hear about world war matters anymore. Reclaiming one's looted art can feel like a Sisyphean task. Masurovsky and his colleagues try to help, but it is always a struggle.

By some estimates around five million cultural heritage objects changed hands inappropriately during the Second World War alone, and that doesn't count the decade leading up to it, when the Nazis were forcibly seizing works of art from their countrymen. Masurovsky considers most estimates published by governments about the number of artworks stolen to be gross underestimates, and he argues quite reasonably that there has been far too much focus on museum-quality masterpieces.

Of course there were tens of thousands of these, including some seven thousand that were destined for Hitler's planned super museum in Linz, Austria, and which were hidden in a salt mine in the Austrian Alps, only to be narrowly rescued from destruction by a team of Austrian miners working with the Resistance, four Austrian double-agent commandos, and the clever work of several of the Monuments Men, as told in my book *Stealing the Mystic Lamb* and partly dramatized in the George Clooney film *Monuments Men*. The sex appeal of headliner masterpieces that were indeed stolen and dramatically recovered (or never recovered and still missing) has led to them overshadowing the millions of objects by significant, but less famous, artists. Masurovsky mentions the likes of Nussbaum and Soutine among the hundreds of Jewish artists who are marginalized, primarily because they were Jewish, even if they were artists of the highest quality.

Masurovsky's initial goal was to raise awareness about issues in restitution, primarily by focusing on archive-trawling research, in order to piece together the ownership histories of objects that changed hands during the Nazi era. But he has also become an activist, much against his will, speaking out on restitution issues as a public figure, because others turn to him for lack of others supporting their cause.

Most of the restitution cases arose during the Internet era, from the late nineties onward, for the simple reason that accessibility of the Internet meant that people, for the first time, knew where certain objects were located, because they could find listings on websites, whereas they would have had to stumble across them in person prior to the Internet's ubiquity to be able to learn their whereabouts. This has led to the children, and now grandchildren, of victims of art plundered during the Second World War bringing lawsuits or seeking the return of objects. Most of the thefts were on the part of the Nazis, but also one of the cofounders of HARP began by specializing in cases in which Allies, while serving in Europe, had quick fingers and took some art back home as souvenirs or trophies.

Unfortunately, what sounds at first like reasonable pleas for the return of looted objects gets complicated quickly. Most cases feature individuals or families, often of limited means, against major institutions like museums or nations. It is far more straightforward if one family is in possession of the work of a family from which that object was likely forcibly removed during the war. But what about when the artwork is now in a national gallery? Deaccessioning a work, particularly from a national collection, is vastly complicated, slow and bureaucratic, even under the best of circumstances with goodwill and desire on all parts. But if museums, or their nations, are resistant, it can be like wading through a tar pit. It is more difficult to find lawyers to help, since such cases rarely involve cash reparations and winnings, normally focused only on ownership of an artwork, so lawyers do not have the same financial incentive to throw themselves into the fray. But just imagine a family of normal middle-class income faced with taking on, say, a national gallery in Austria, in order to claim a painting that was once owned by their ancestor. The cards are stacked wildly in favor of such megalithic institutions, with extensive boards of trustees and staff lawyers and sometimes ministries backing them up. It is daunting, to say the least, and most potential claimants give up in the early stages, scared by the prospects.

HARP put their names on the map by pointing out to the District Attorney's Office of New York the fact that two paintings by Egon Schiele, on loan from Austria, had questionable backgrounds and yet were sent to MoMA in New York for display in an exhibition. After HARP sounded the alarm, the district attorney determined that it would hear a case for the restitution of these two paintings to two separate Jewish families that claimed that they had been taken from them. The seizure of the paintings in that case led directly to Austria implementing a new law on restitution, the first European country to do so. Masurovsky says, with a sigh, that it seems that a fight must be undertaken in the courtroom, for anyone to pay attention and make changes.

The very fact that the courtroom seems to be the only place that prompts useful action is proof enough that the Washington Principles, while well-meaning, have been ineffectual.

The Washington Principles on Nazi-Confiscated Art were published on December 3, 1998. Part of the Washington Conference on Holocaust-Era Assets, they were a declaration, primarily written by Stuart Eizenstat, that outlined how to deal with restitution claims. They offered "nonbinding principles," which is to say that they were merely suggestions, "without any teeth," as Masurovsky says. While clearly well-meaning, they appear to have a great deal of weight and pomp, but as the experts with whom I spoke for this essay collectively agreed, they don't really do anything, and so are not useful to claimants. Masurovsky, in his thoughtful blog, *Plundered Art*, offers suggestions that would update them, but he is wary of the conference scheduled for November 2018 in Berlin, commemorating twenty years of the Washington Principles. It may involve much self-congratulation about something that has had almost no actual positive effect.

Masurovsky cites numerous high-profile cases in which major museums, often backed by their nations, refused to return objects that were demonstrably looted. It is ironic, for instance, that the Brera Museum in Milan refuses to return a painting from the Gentile collection, when the nation of Italy has repeatedly and successfully demanded the restitution of ancient artworks looted from its territory. Yet, if they possess a painting that was demonstrably looted from a Jewish family, they don't want to hear about returning it. This is a point that even the former advocate general of Italy, Maurizio Fiorilli, agreed with, when he met with me and Masurovsky at the recent ARCA Conference on the Study of Art Crime, that is held every summer in Italy and which has become the mean annual meeting place for specialists in the field. Sometimes even nations, whom we tend to think of as working the best for their citizens, have dug their heels in. Masurovsky says that Switzerland only last year organized the restitution of a war-looted artwork, making it seven decades after the fact, and with numerous other possible objects not restituted (or at least, not yet). And things are not looking up. Masurovsky mentions that the Netherlands has recently changed the rules for restituting looted art, stating that they will consider restitutions from museums if removing the questioned object would not interfere with the museum's didactic program. This gives museums a "Get Out of Jail Free Card," refusing reasonable restitution claims on the grounds that it will "mess up" their exhibition layout. This is something that Masurovsky cannot abide, and one can see why. The most difficult element that Masurovsky sees as a stumbling block in legitimate restitutions is current owners hiding behind the claim of "good faith purchases." According to current law, one must only be able to demonstrate that you genuinely thought an object was legitimate when you acquired it, and one is unlikely to be required to return the object in question, much less suffer any legal damages. One can imagine that it is relatively easy to claim good faith, even if one's faith was not good. This has been the undoing of many cases. But for the thousands of cases in which the victims gave up, for fear of the uphill battle, before they really got started, or the scores of important cases that were heard, Masurovsky and his colleagues have been there, behind the scenes and sometimes at the fore, traveling the world to speak about this cause, occasionally appearing in courtrooms, and talking about the dangers of provenance research.

Why dangerous? "Because provenance has become a political tool," he says. Attempting to research provenance means looking into the often-unseemly past of nations, and sometimes their heroes, whether they are museums or politicians and art world protagonists. Does America really want to learn that some of their so-called "Monuments Men," who have been so glorified for their efforts to save Europe's art treasures, may have also pocketed some of them? Does Germany want to uncover still more unseemly tales of its recent history? Does amiable Switzerland want to hear in the courts of some of its less-amiable activities or oversights from decades past? These are things that people and even nations feel like they would often rather forget, but it is just these stories that are most important and are where the keys lie to unlocking and solving long-ago mysteries involving some of the world's most beautiful art.

How Did ISIS Inadvertently Uncover a Link to One of the Lost Seven Wonders of the Ancient World?

In 2017, a group of concerned archaeologists, mapping out the extent of the damage wrought by ISIS when they occupied the Iraqi city of Mosul, announced a shocking discovery. Back in 2014, the terrorist group had gleefully announced their destruction of the Nebi Yunus shrine, traditionally believed to be the tomb of the prophet Jonah, and a part of the ancient ruins of the city of Nineveh. In February of 2017 the Iraqi Army drove ISIS out of Mosul, giving archaeologists their first chance to inspect the devastation. ISIS's funding of their activities through the sale of illicit antiquities is well-documented. Anything they might find, in the course of their plowing through ancient sites, would be gathered for sale abroad, while they would destroy as much as they could along the way, documenting the harm in order to upset their ideological enemies.

At first there was little concern that Nineveh would yield saleable artifacts. It had been carefully excavated by waves of archaeologists since at least 1842. The only chance of finding new treasures would be to search where no one has looked before. And the only place no one has looked, where archaeologists would not try to look, would be places which can only be accessed by blowing up or bulldozing the already-revealed parts of the ancient city.

To the surprise of the archaeologists, upon examining the reconquered city, they found evidence that when ISIS blew up parts of the Nebi Yunus shrine, they had unveiled a major discovery: a palace that predated the tomb of Jonah, and had been buried beneath it, unseen for thousands of years.

In terms of exposing history, this is a major find. But ISIS got there first and, as archaeologist Layla Salih said, "I can only imagine how much Daesh [ISIS] discovered down there before we got here." On the other hand, optimism was reinjected when she and her team found some items of great interest (and value) that had not been taken. For example, there is an inscribed piece of marble with cuneiform that includes turns of phrase used elsewhere exclusively to describe a specific king, Esarhaddon, ruler of Assyria circa 672 BC.

This suggests that the newly discovered seventh-century BC palace is one that historians knew of but thought long lost: one begun by King Sennacherib and completed by his son, Esarhaddon. This palace was so badly damaged during the 612 BC sack of Nineveh, a loss at the hands of an allied army that ended the Neo-Assyrian Empire, that it was never occupied again. Components of it were reused in other, new buildings, once the city was reconstructed. Buildings like the tomb of Jonah.

But the story doesn't end there. It's in fact a poetically linked component in a chain of lost monuments and ancient kings, dating back to one of the Seven Wonders of the Ancient World, the only one that historians have wondered if it ever existed at all.

You can still visit the Great Pyramid at Giza today. But all of the other Seven Wonders are known to have been destroyed. All except for the Hanging Gardens of Babylon. The presence and loss of the others are accounted for in archaeological and historical documentation: the Tomb of Mausolus, the Lighthouse of Alexandria, the Temple of Artemis at Ephesus, the Colossus of Rhodes, and the Statue of Zeus at Olympia.

The gardens were meant to have been a series of tiers, a sort of ziggurat-like step-pyramid planted with all manner of greenery at each level but lined also with colonnades. Because there are no known Babylonian texts that refer to the gardens, which is odd considering how magnificent and noteworthy they were meant to have been, some have thought that they might be just a legend. The idea of seeing Seven Wonders was popularized by ancient Greek and Roman travel writers. But they were writing about wonders that were already ancient to them, centuries old, and they were writing circa 100 BC to 100 AD. Thus their own knowledge was based on hearsay, rather than firsthand examination.

The story of the Hanging Gardens is pieced together through fractious accounts of these various ancient historians. It goes something like this: A king, possibly Nebuchadnezzar II (who ruled 605–562 BC), built the gardens for his wife, Queen Amytis, who missed the green landscape of her home in Media (northern Iran). While classical writers described the gardens, it is unlikely that any of them actually saw them. The most specific description comes from Diodorus Siculus (active 60–30 BC). He wrote that the garden was around four hundred feet on each side, and "sloped like a hillside and the several parts of the structure rose from one another, tier on tier, the appearance of the whole resembling a theater." The highest tier stood twenty meters high, "level with the circuit wall of the battlements of the city." The walls were twenty-two feet thick, with walkways ten feet wide. Diodorus described the structure of the gardens as made of brick bonded with cement, then topped with bitumen (an ancient version of asphalt) and a layer of lead "to the end that the moisture from the soil might not penetrate beneath," then piled with soil and "thickly planted with trees of every kind that, by their great size or other charm, could give pleasure to the beholder." The detail offered suggests the description of a real place, though Diodorus wrote that a Syrian king built it, not a Babylonian one, just to confuse matters. A first-century AD Roman writer, Quintus Curtius Rufus, described a similar structure, further lending credence to its onetime existence.

But recent scholars, like Stephanie Daley, suggest that this garden of Babylon might actually have been conflated with a garden that did indeed exist, for which archaeological evidence is available: a famous garden built not in Babylon but by the destroyer of Babylon, Assyrian king Sennacherib, for his capital in Nineveh. That's right, the same king who started the palace that was just discovered thanks to ISIS's iconoclasm.

Some ancient sources also seem to enforce this hypothesis, through exclusion rather than inclusion. It's weird, for instance, that Herodotus, when describing Babylon, does not mention the Hanging Gardens. This suggests that it was never in that city to begin with.

Meanwhile, in Nineveh, archaeologists found an eighty-kilometer (fifty-mile) network of waterways (aqueducts, canals, dams) which carried water to the desert city, where a series of water-raising screws brought the water uphill to irrigate the gardens. If the famous Hanging Garden was never in Babylon, but was actually the one in Nineveh, then it does not qualify as lost at all—its remnants can be visited today. If a similar such garden once existed in Babylon, then it might have been damaged, destroyed, or its materials reused over millennia of invaders overtaking the ancient city (including an Assyrian period, during which engineers might have been inspired to create the gardens of Nineveh).

The picture grows more intriguing, as it was King Sennacherib, the man who commissioned the Nineveh gardens and ruled Assyria from 705 to 681 BC, who ordered the destruction of all the defensive walls, palaces, and temples of Babylon as a deterrent to the regular uprising of the population against the Assyrian conquerors. If they were there at all, it was then, in 689 BC, that the gardens met their fate—possibly only to be "rebuilt" in Nineveh, maybe even with elements dismantled and transferred to the Assyrian capital. But it remains entirely possible that they were never in Babylon at all, and that instead they should have been called the Hanging Gardens of Nineveh, built by the king who razed Babylon and raised a palace there that was just discovered, thanks to the iconoclastic hands of ISIS.

Napoleon: Emperor of Art Theft

When Citizen Wicar, one of the key members of the art theft division of Napoleon's army, died in 1834, he bequeathed 1,436 artworks as a gift to his birthplace, the city of Lille. Though most were works on paper (prints and drawings), this is an astonishing number. But there are two more facts about this bit of historical trivia that make it that much more surprising. First, almost all of these works had been stolen by him, personally, over the course of his service to the Napoleonic Army, in which he and several other officers were charged with selecting, removing, boxing up, and shipping back to Paris art from the collections of those vanquished by La Grande Armée. Stealing over a thousand artworks is no small feat for a single person, even with the sort of unrestricted access his position with the army allowed. Impressive enough, until we reach the second fact: Citizen Wicar had already sold most of the art he had stolen over the course of his postwar life, but he still had those thousand-odd pieces left over to bequeath. In terms of quantity, Citizen Wicar, who would serve as Keeper of Antiquities at the Louvre Museum, is the most prolific art thief in history. But it is his boss, Napoleon Bonaparte, who is often crowned with that title.

Organized looting by Napoleon's army began with the conditions of the armistice signed May 17, 1796, after he had defeated the Duke of Modena: "The Duke of Modena undertakes to hand over twenty pictures. They will be selected by commissioners sent for that purpose from among the pictures in his gallery and realm." This set a precedent for payment and reparations in the form of artworks that would enrage and dismay surrendering peoples for centuries to come.

Napoleon gave strict instructions on the proper removal of artworks. Special agents were ordered to use the army to commandeer art, arrange transport to France, and make a precise inventory. This inventory was to be presented to the army commander and the government attaché to the army. Records of each confiscation were to be made in the presence of a French Army–recognized official. Army transport was to be used to bring loot back to France and the army was to cover the costs. In fact, these careful instructions served to veil the personal circumvention of them by Napoleon and his officers.

The coyly named Commission of Arts and Sciences was led by an artist, Citizen Tinet, and consisted of a mathematician, Citizen Monge, a botanist called Citizen Thouin, and another painter, Citizen Wicar—the most notorious of the lot, who proved to be a thief for the ages.

Napoleon was not much of an art connoisseur. But luckily for him (and unluckily for those he subdued), Napoleon had a powerful and cunning art advisor: the first director of the Louvre Museum, Dominique-Vivant Denon.

Denon had served as an artist to the court of King Louis XV, gave drawing lessons to the king's mistress, Madame de Pompadour, acted as ambassador to the court of Catherine the Great in Russia and in Naples. But he is best known as the man who turned the Louvre from a residential palace of the deposed French monarchy into the world's most famous art gallery. He was the Louvre's first director (and a wing is still named after him). We owe much of how we think about museums today to Denon's legacy: he was the first to curate a museum by style (Baroque Italian paintings all in one room); to attempt to put together an encyclopedic collection, covering the whole history of art; and to hang striking works so that they are framed by doorways and can be seen from a distance, drawing the eye; among other innovations. In a letter to Napoleon in 1803, the year after he became the first director of the Louvre, he described the need for this museum to feature the best works from "the Renaissance of the arts until our own time." In this way, the museum should provide "a history course in the art of painting," presenting its collection with "a character of order, instruction, and classification." He had become Napoleon's personal art advisor after having caught his eye, when he accompanied the general on his 1798 Egyptian campaign, sketching pyramids while the cannons were still warm. Denon saw Napoleon's attempt to reconquer the extent of the Roman Empire as a chance to bring together the greatest artworks of the vanquished territories. He drew up an art historian's dream wish list of works that he would love to have at the Louvre, and the army's art theft unit, featuring the nimble-fingered Citizen Wicar, sought to fill it. If Denon was the ur-connoisseur, Napoleon was anything but. As Andrew Roberts explains in his biography, *Napoleon: A Life*, the general's main criteria for whether he liked a work was its size (the bigger the better) and its naturalism (if it looked like real life, then it must be good). But this suited Denon just fine—he was happy for Napoleon to appropriate oversized academic realist works for his personal enjoyment, as long as the choicest, most important works went to the Louvre. Denon would accompany Napoleon on most of his later campaigns, advising on which artworks to confiscate and send to the Louvre. His nickname was *l'emballeur*, "the packer," for his constant supervision of the packing and shipping to Paris of looted artworks.

Both Denon and Napoleon were great enthusiasts of their looting schemes. For example, on October 1, 1803, when one hundred cases packed full of antiquities (including the *Medici Venus* and the *Capitoline Venus*) looted from Italy arrived at the Louvre without a single object broken en route,

Denon excitedly made a speech calling Napoleon "the hero of our century, [who] during the torment of war, required of our enemies trophies of peace, and he has seen to their conservation." Stealing art from defeated enemies as an act of conservation.

When Napoleon became emperor in 1804, Denon was made Inspector General of French Museums, ostensibly the director of all national collections. Both he and Napoleon understood that there was symbolic power in the capture and display of the cultural treasures of fallen nations. There was historical precedent for this: art had been looted by conquering armies for as long as one could remember, but it was seen as acceptable because the ancient Romans did it. Indeed, the city of Rome was decorated with looted statues, including an outdoor sculpture garden once located near to where the Ghetto is today, all of its content stolen. Looted art is like a battle flag, displayed by the victors to demonstrate who they have vanquished: a more elegant and enduring version of exhibiting the severed heads of enemy generals.

The Louvre—originally known as the Musée Français, then the Musée Central des Arts, then the Musée Napoleon from 1803 to 1814, before becoming the Musée du Louvre—became a popular pilgrimage point for the cultured traveler. The accumulation of looted art in Paris was a constant point of discussion in European publications and elicited a great deal of interest in what might be called "illicit art tourism."

In 1802 Henry Milton, an Englishman traveling to Paris specifically to see the loot-stocked Louvre, wrote: "Bands of practiced robbers who could not find an outlet for their talents in their homeland were shipped abroad to commit crimes under another, less discreditable name. . . . Hordes of thieves in the form of experts and connoisseurs accompanied their armies to take possession, either by dictation or naked force, of all that seemed to them worth taking."

Napoleon's art theft unit was established with whitewashed intentions. In June 1794, he established a "Committee for the Education of the People" and proposed sending "knowledgeable civilians with our armies, with confidential instructions to seek out and obtain the works of art in the countries invaded by us." On July 18, 1794, the following order was issued to the army: "The People's commissioners with the Armies of the North and Sambre-et-Meuse have learned that in the territories invaded by the victorious armies of the French Republic in order to expel the hirelings of the tyrants there are works of painting and sculpture and other products of genius. They are of the opinion that the proper place for them, in the interests and for the honor of art, is in the home of free men."

Citizen Wicar and others in the unit oversaw the selection, boxing, and shipping of art from collections after ceasefires had been signed. But in practice, a lot more looting took place than was mandated by treaties. Napoleon at least put on a front of attempting to keep it in check.

In an order on April 22, 1796, Napoleon stated: "The Commander-in-Chief commends the army for its bravery and for the victories it has wrested from the enemy day after day." He sees with horror, however, the dreadful looting committed by pathetic individuals who only join their units when the fighting is over, because they have been busy looting.

The soldiers paid little heed. Shortly thereafter, Napoleon issued this order: "The Commander-in-Chief is informed that in spite of repeated orders, looting in the army continues, and houses in the countryside are stripped," that any soldier found looting will be shot, and that no objects may be confiscated without written permission of specified authorities. But in the heat of the campaign, this was heeded little, least of all by Napoleon, who made a habit of showing up at galleries and choosing works that he liked for his own collection.

Napoleon was as enthusiastic as Denon, when it came to looting. As he wound his way through the Italian Peninsula, he extracted thousands of artworks from those who opposed him. Recognizing this inevitability, Turin and Naples determined not to engage in combat, and so they were far less looted than others who dug in to fight. Pope Pius VI agreed to terms with Napoleon in June 1796, but he paid heavily. In addition to the payment of twenty-one million livres in money and goods (approximately $60 million today), Article 8 of the Treaty of Tolentine stated that the Pope was to hand over: "A hundred pictures, busts, vases or statues to be selected by the commissioners and sent to Rome, including in particular the bronze bust of Junius Brutus and the marble bust of Marcus Brutus, both on the Capitol, also five hundred manuscripts at the choice of the said commissioners."

Adding insult to injury, the Vatican was required to pay for the transport of all of the art forced from it by the French, for an astonishing sum of eight hundred thousand livres, about $3.6 million today. Forty paintings were taken from Papal dominion in Bologna and ten more from Ferrara. In total, the looted art of Bologna alone required eighty-six wagons to transport. Napoleon wrote with overt glee: "The Commission of experts has made a fine haul in Ravenna, Rimini, Pesaro, Ancona, Loretto, and Perugia. The whole lot will be forwarded to Paris without delay. There is also the consignment from Rome itself. We have stripped Italy of everything of artistic worth, with the exception of a few objects in Turin and Naples!"

Walk through the Louvre today, and one can still find works that entered the collection thanks to Napoleon, Denon, Wicar, and their like. When you look at Jan van Eyck's *Madonna with Canon van der Paele* (looted in 1794 from what was then called the Austrian Netherlands, modern Belgium), consider the legacy of Napoleonic looting, but also the power of Denon, the true mastermind behind the second-largest art theft scheme in history—to which we owe a great deal in terms of how we think about art, the breadth of great collections, and how museums function.

Napoleon and Denon's legacies would likewise resonate through the twentieth century and inspire the only art thief who outdid them in scope. Prior to the First World War, international newspapers warned of the need never to repeat the art looting seen under Napoleon. That sounded well and good, but when the bullets started flying, theory was not put into practice. Art was looted, damaged, and destroyed during the First World War, but it was not until the Second that Napoleon was very much outdone.

Hitler established his own art theft unit, the ERR (Einsatzstab Reichsleiter Rosenberg), inspired by Napoleon, which focused on seizing art, books, and documents that were of "value" to the Third Reich. By some estimates around five million cultural heritage objects (a term that includes fine art but extends well beyond it) were stolen, looted, or destroyed. While Napoleon and Denon envisioned the Louvre as a sort of encyclopedic super museum, Hitler had a similar vision that was very nearly realized. He planned to rebuild the majority of his boyhood hometown of Linz, Austria, and make it into a citywide museum containing every important artwork in the world. He used the ERR to fill a wish list of his own, focused on his preference for Teutonic and Scandinavian artists and subject matter. The seven thousand choicest works, stolen from throughout conquered Europe and destined for the Linz museum, were stored in a secret salt mine in the Austrian Alps. They were nearly all destroyed when a local SS leader determined to blow up the mine and its contents, if he could not defend it against the encroaching Allies. While Napoleon oversaw the looting of tens of thousands of works, Hitler reached the hundreds of thousands, and far more met unseemly fates due to his policies and campaigns. If there is a hell for art thieves, then surely Hitler and Napoleon share the throne.

The British Origin of the Monuments Men

Since 2014, when George Clooney's drama came out about the Monuments Men and their adventures in saving Europe's art treasures during the Second World War, viewers have become privy to a Hollywoodization of a true, dramatic, epic story of the race to rescue an estimated five million cultural heritage objects, from paintings and sculptures to rare books and valuable archival materials, that were looted by the Nazis and risked complete destruction. The Clooney film is only loosely based on historical fact—it necessarily compresses, condenses, and alters reality to fit the rules of a Hollywood feature. But one aspect of the Monuments Men that most American accounts skip past or exclude altogether is the fact that they began as a British operation—its spearhead was a most British brand of hero, Sir Leonard Woolley.

The Monuments Men was the nickname of a group of some three hundred Allied officers, members of the art world during their civilian lives (architects, conservators, archaeologists, art historians) who were charged with identifying art and monuments that might be in the line of fighting in Europe during the Second World War. Once these works, from Notre Dame Cathedral to the entire contents of the Uffizi, were identified, the officers would advise the Allied armies they accompanied on how, whenever possible, to avoid damage to these cultural monuments. That part of their call of duty was the British plan. But their role changed in practice, once the officers were in the field and it became clear, only late in the war, that there was an enormous, proactive art-looting plan that the Nazis had put into operation, led by their art theft unit, the ERR, and intended to both enrich the Nazi war effort and fill Hitler's planned "super museum" that would occupy the entirety of his boyhood town of Linz, Austria, which would contain every important artwork in the world. Once in the field, as an underappreciated and undersupported twig attached to the massive Allied armies, the Monuments Men began to act as wartime art detectives, seeking out key stolen works, piecing together clues as to the overall Nazi art theft plan, and eventually rescuing tens of thousands of looted masterpieces, including van Eyck's *Adoration of the Mystic Lamb* and Michelangelo's *Bruges Madonna*—the twin focal points of the Clooney film.

In anticipation of *The Monuments Men* film, much was written about them, but what tends to go overlooked is the role that British scholar-soldiers had in establishing the very idea that scholars could aide warriors in the collective goal of protecting the world's cultural heritage.

It was the British who first recognized, early in the war, the need for a division of officers trained in, and dedicated to, the protection of art and monuments in conflict zones. In January 1943, during a pause in the fighting near Tripoli in North Africa, Mortimer Wheeler, the director of the London Museum and a renowned archaeologist, grew concerned about the fate of three ruined ancient cities nearby along the coast of Libya: Sabratha, Leptis Magna, and Oea (the ancient city around which Tripoli grew). With the impending defeat of the Axis in North Africa, and the chaos of the war, Wheeler worried that the ancient monuments could become "easy meat for any dog that came along."

Wheeler noted with concern that there was no system of any sort in place for the Allies to safeguard any archives, artworks, museums, or monuments in their path.

Wheeler grabbed a friend and fellow officer, a famous British art historian and archaeologist in his own right, John Ward-Perkins, and they drove by jeep to the sites of Oea and Leptis Magna. Leptis Magna, birthplace of the emperor Septimius Severus, had recently been excavated by a team of Italian archaeologists under Mussolini's orders. This meant that the marvels of the ancient architecture, and even statuary, were unearthed but had not been secured and moved to museums. When they arrived, Wheeler and Ward-Perkins were dismayed to find a Royal Air Force team setting up a radar station in the ruins, which they thought would provide good cover.

The two archaeologists pretended to have an authority they did not possess. As Ward-Perkins would later write, "We bluffed our way through a number of fairly effective measures." They improvised "Out of Bounds" signs, which they mounted on key monuments and beside statues, and they began to provide informal lectures to troops about their surroundings, to instill a sense of respect and appreciation for the ruins and artworks around them. These measures would become standard procedure for the Monuments, Fine Arts, and Archives Division, colloquially called the Monuments Men, the division that their actions would in part inspire.

In June 1943, Wheeler decided to use his impressive list of contacts to make something official out of their improvised policy. He was spurred on by his knowledge of the planned Allied invasion of Sicily, which Wheeler described as "a top secret to which I happened to be a party. The archaeologist in me was filled with anxiety." One of the richest places on earth, archaeologically and artistically, Sicily's treasures were in serious danger if something was not done in anticipation of the invasion. Wheeler suggested that a small, well-organized group, led by a qualified archaeologist, be established to promote the protection of monuments in Sicily. This message eventually reached Secretary of State for War Sir P. J. Grigg and Prime Minister Winston Churchill himself. Agreeing with the idea, they immediately sought out an archaeologist to lead the operation.

Enter Sir Leonard Woolley. In October 1943, the British established a division of the War Office, the Archaeological Adviser's Branch that would deal with the recovery and protection of art objects in newly liberated territories. It was originally a one-man operation, run by Woolley, who was already a renowned archaeologist, with his wife as his only assistant. Woolley liked it that way, rejecting the offer of staff. He liked to think that his uncluttered judgment was far superior to what a committee could produce, and he wanted to be able to boast of the triumphs he'd achieved, ostensibly alone. In truth, he was a brilliant archaeologist and politician. The son of a clergyman, Woolley was a curator at Oxford's Ashmolean Museum and was best known for leading archaeological excavations at Ur (in present-day Iraq), but he had also worked alongside T. E. Lawrence in Syria, in 1913. The budding novelist Agatha Christie was a great admirer of Woolley, particularly noting his capacity to galvanize listeners about the wonders of archaeology. (Christie spent a lot of time with Woolley—she even married Woolley's assistant from his Ur excavation, in 1930.) Christie wrote, "Leonard Woolley saw with the eye of the imagination. Wherever we happened to be, he could make it come alive. It was his reconstruction of the past and he believed it, and anyone who listened believed it also."

When the war began, Woolley corresponded with various relevant institutions to compile lists of artworks and monuments in the path of the fighting. He eventually began to recruit personnel, as it became clear that a field force would be needed to accompany Allied armies, though he did so very much against his will. Woolley thought that his role, and therefore the role of anyone working in the sphere of the protection of art and monuments, should be to note sites for the army to avoid, and to plan for the restitution of art and artifacts after the war—not to send out field officers. He wrote, "The idea that we should leave the most eminent experts who have high artistic or archaeological qualifications to walk about the battlefields for this purpose is really one which I think would not be accepted as at all suitable." There was an element of classism in this statement—the lives of the highly educated should not be risked in combat zones—in addition to the desire to be the one and only operator in the tiny, newly founded "theater" of art and archaeological protection during war. It would take a strong American push to dislodge Woolley's hands-off policy and encourage Allied fieldwork in the protection of art and monuments.

Over the course of Woolley's operations, intelligence established that art was being confiscated in all Nazi-occupied territories, including the art of German citizens, and that stolen art, through barter and sale abroad, provided one of the largest economic assets of the Reich.

In May 1944, a larger sister division was organized by direct command of Winston Churchill. Under the supervision of Lord Hugh Pattison Macmillan, the verbosely named British Committee on Preservation and Restitution of Works of Art, Archives, and Other Material in Enemy Hands was established. This rather unwieldy nomenclature was cast aside in favor of the simpler Macmillan Committee. The Macmillan Committee would now be in charge of the planned postwar restitution of looted works of art, with Woolley acting as their civilian leader. Woolley's motto was "We protect the arts at the lowest possible cost," an odd banner under which to fight, but one that was, at least initially, politically necessary in order to garner support for a role that was considered of secondary importance by the majority. Meanwhile, the United States was forming its own art protection divisions. As early as March 1941, the United States had established the Committee on Conservation of Cultural Resources, designed to protect and conserve art in American collections from the perceived impending threat of Japanese invasion, after the December 1941 attack on Pearl Harbor.

Early on during the war, certain art organizations, including the American Harvard Defense Group and the American Council of Learned Societies, had worked with museums and art historians to identify European monuments and artworks that would require protection. These groups began to lobby for a national organization for the preservation of cultural properties during times of war. Much of this was led by Paul Sachs, director of the Harvard Fogg Museum, and by Francis Henry Taylor, director of the Metropolitan Museum of Art. Both members of American blue-blooded "aristocracy," they were incredibly well-connected and used this to their advantage, calling on such friends as President Franklin D. Roosevelt himself.

At their encouragement, Roosevelt eventually brought into being the American Commission for the Protection and Salvage of Artistic and Historic Monuments in War Areas, established June 23, 1943. This committee was chaired by Supreme Court Justice Owen J. Roberts and, therefore, became known as the Roberts Commission. By the summer of 1943, the Roberts Commission had finished 168 maps covering all of Italy, its islands, and even the Dalmatian coast. A total of some seven hundred maps would be produced, covering all of Europe, including detail maps of the major cities, and a significant number of Asian cities, as well.

The Roberts Commission was further charged with protecting cultural properties in conflict zones, provided that their preservation did not impede active and necessary military operations. To do so, it established the Monuments, Fine Arts, and Archives branch of the Civil Affairs and Military Government sections of the Allied armies, to act as their agents in the field, referred to as the MFAA or the Monuments Men.

The establishment of the Monuments Men was a significant victory in what had become a tug-of-egos between the laissez-faire Sir Leonard Woolley, working largely alone in England, and the huge committee of American art historians and museum directors, led by Francis Henry Taylor. Woolley lobbied with the War Office in England not to send out field officers, and at first succeeded—the Macmillan Committee only handled restitution of displaced artworks after the war. But it was not quite as Woolley hoped, as he was obliged to act as British representative to the Roberts Commission, which prepped the Monuments Men for fieldwork.

Despite support from presidents, prime ministers, and General Dwight Eisenhower, from the start the Monuments Men were sidelined and often dismissed by the commanders of the Allied armies. It was a well-meaning but undersupported and incompletely conceived effort that wound up frustrating its officers. With limited infrastructure and support (often without transport, having to hitchhike from one site to the next), they did the best they could. Their practical actions were largely based on the policies that Wheeler and Ward-Perkins had improvised, back at Leptis Magna in 1943.

Despite their handicaps in terms of support, equipment, and status within the Allied armies, we have the Monuments Men to thank for some truly astonishing recoveries. The most famous of all is the improbable and miraculous salvation of the twelve thousand masterpieces that were stored in a secret art warehouse in a salt mine in the Austrian Alps, at Altaussee.

Thanks to the bravery of Austrian miners working with the Resistance, a Woolley-inspired team of Austrian double-agent commandos, Monuments Men Robert Posey and Lincoln Kirstein, and a fortuitous toothache, these works, by artists from van Eyck to Michelangelo, Leonardo to Vermeer, Titian to Rembrandt, destined for Hitler's planned Linz museum, were all saved from a renegade SS officer determined to blow them all up, if he could not defend them against the Allies.

When *The Monuments Men* film came out, it hopefully inspired a good many viewers to turn to the true story of this unique division of admirable officers who loved art enough to risk their lives for it. One of their number, the British scholar Ronald Balfour, was one of two Monuments Men who died during service (though not in the melodramatic way depicted in the film). His words are a fitting end to our story which, it must be remembered, began as a British affair: "If these [artworks] are lost or broken or destroyed, we lose a valuable part of our knowledge about our forefathers. No age lives entirely alone; every civilization is formed not merely by its own achievements, but by what it has inherited from the past. If these things are destroyed, we have lost a part of our past, and we shall be the poorer for it."

Suggestions for Further Reading

As noted, this collection intentionally has no citations, since all of its chapters were intended for general readers and many were first published in popular newspapers and magazines. There are too many diverse subjects to make a bibliography practical. For more details, citations, and a proper bibliography, I would point you to my other books on this subject, to past issues of the *Journal of Art Crime*, as well as to some books I've contributed to in some way (writing a foreword, encouraging the author, penning a chapter, and such).

Bruinsma, Gerben, ed. *Histories of Transnational Crime*. New York: Springer, 2015.

Charney, Noah, ed. *Art and Crime: Exploring the Dark Side of the Art World*. Westport, CT: Praeger, 2009.

Charney, Noah, ed. *Art Crime: Terrorists, Tomb Raiders, Forgers and Thieves*. New York: Palgrave Macmillan, 2016.

Charney, Noah. *The Art of Forgery*. New York: Phaidon, 2015.

Charney, Noah. *The Devil in the Gallery: How Scandal, Shock, and Rivalry Made the Art World*. Lanham, MD: Rowman & Littlefield, 2019.

Charney, Noah. *The Museum of Lost Art*. New York: Phaidon, 2018.

Charney, Noah. *Stealing the Mystic Lamb: The True Story of the World's Most Coveted Masterpiece*. New York: PublicAffairs, 2010.

Charney, Noah. *The Thefts of the* Mona Lisa*: The Complete Story of the World's Most Famous Painting*. Lanham, MD: Rowman & Littlefield, 2024.

Charney, Noah, and Ingrid Rowland. *Collector of Lives: Giorgio Vasari and the Invention of Art*. New York: W. W. Norton, 2017.

Charney, Noah, and Kenny Schachter. *The NFT Book: Everything You Need to Know about the Art and Collecting of Non-Fungible Tokens*. Lanham, MD: Rowman & Littlefield, 2023.

Hirsch, Alan. *The Duke of Wellington, Kidnapped! The Incredible True Story of the Art Heist That Shocked a Nation*. Berkeley, CA: Counterpoint, 2017.

Hufnagel, Saskia, and Duncan Chappell, ed. *Contemporary Perspectives on the Detection, Investigation and Prosecution of Art Crime*. Farnham, UK: Ashgate, 2014.

Hufnagel, Saskia, and Duncan Chappell, ed. *The Palgrave Handbook on Art Crime*. New York: Palgrave Macmillan, 2019.
Moses, Nancy. *Fakes, Forgeries, and Frauds*. Lanham, MD: Rowman & Littlefield, 2020.
Tompkins, Arthur, ed. *Art Crime and Its Prevention*. London: Lund Humphries, 2016.

INDEX

About the Author

Noah Charney, PhD, is the internationally best-selling author of more than a dozen books, translated into fourteen languages, including *The Collector of Lives: Giorgio Vasari and the Invention of Art*, which was nominated for the 2017 Pulitzer Prize in Biography, and *The Museum of Lost Art*, which was a finalist for the 2018 Digital Book World Award. He is a professor of art history specializing in art crime and has taught at Yale University, Brown University, American University of Rome, and University of Ljubljana. He is founder of ARCA, the Association for Research into Crimes against Art, a groundbreaking research group (www.artcrimeresearch.org), and teaches in their annual summer-long Postgraduate Program in Art Crime and Cultural Heritage Protection. He has written for dozens of major magazines and newspapers, including the *Guardian*, the *Washington Post*, the *Observer*, and the *Art Newspaper*. His recent books on art include *The Devil in the Gallery: How Scandal, Shock, and Rivalry Shaped the Art World*, *Making It: The Artist's Survival Guide*, *The 12-Hour Art Expert: Everything You Need to Know about Art in a Dozen Masterpieces*, and *Brushed Aside: The Untold Story of Women in Art*, several of which were Amazon number one bestsellers in their category. He also published the critically acclaimed *Slavic Myths* (2023) and *The Thefts of the* Mona Lisa*: The Complete Story of the World's Most Famous Artwork* (2024), which was praised in the *New York Times Book Review* and the *Telegraph*, among others. He recently fronted an influencer campaign for Samsung; in 2022 he presented a BBC Radio 4 documentary, *China's Stolen Treasures*; his TED Ed videos (some on art crime) have been viewed by millions each; and he featured in a recent Amazon Prime documentary, *The Picasso of Thieves*. A course of his, Lost Art, features in The Teaching Company's Great Courses/Wondrium, the first of several that are scheduled, and he teaches online courses for Atlas Obscura, the Smithsonian, the National Gallery (UK), and Yale University on art theft and forgery. He lives in Slovenia with his wife, children, and their hairless dog, Hubert van Eyck (believe it or not). Learn more at www.noahcharney.com.

www.ingramcontent.com/pod-product-compliance
Lightning Source LLC
LaVergne TN
LVHW090520110826
845146LV00003B/934

9798881802639